Nurturing Children through the Primary Years

This book argues that supporting a child's learning in primary school is more about nurturing their dispositions than continually assessing their performance. Drawing on the latest research in the fields of child development, psychology, health and well-being, it shows how teachers and parents have a deep impact on children's learning, motivation and potential and the practices that offer children the best opportunities for future success.

Guided by the holistic approaches of the Nurturing Childhoods Pedagogical Framework and the ABCs of Developing Engagement, this book has a strong focus on increasing child engagement alongside methods to consider the impact of learning experiences.

Chapters cover:

■ Supporting engagement through communication, movement and play

■ Helping children to feel safe and secure within their learning environments

■ Developing classrooms where children think and express themselves

■ Understanding childhood anxiety

■ Nurturing confidence and self-motivation

■ Working with parents and carers

■ Anxiety within the classroom

■ Ways of evaluating teaching styles and class dynamics

■ Decoding children's behaviours

Part of the *Nurturing Childhoods* series, this exciting book provides teachers, practitioners and parents with the knowledge and understanding they need to nurture children's happiness, well-being and sense of security throughout their school years.

Kathryn Peckham is a Childhood Consultant, researcher, author and founder of Nurturing Childhoods. She is an active member of global Early Childhood networks, conducting research for governments and international organisations, writing curricula and contributing to industry leading publications and guidance such as Birth to 5 Matters.

Nurturing Children through the Primary Years

Developing the Potential of Every Child

Kathryn Peckham

Routledge
Taylor & Francis Group

LONDON AND NEW YORK

Designed cover image: © Getty Images

First published 2025
by Routledge
4 Park Square, Milton Park, Abingdon, Oxon, OX14 4RN

and by Routledge
605 Third Avenue, New York, NY 10158

Routledge is an imprint of the Taylor & Francis Group, an informa business

British Library Cataloguing-in-Publication Data
A catalogue record for this book is available from the British Library

Library of Congress Cataloging-in-Publication Data
Names: Peckham, Kathryn, author.
Title: Nurturing children through the primary years : developing the potential of every child / Kathryn Peckham.
Description: Abingdon, Oxon ; New York, NY : Routledge, 2025. | Includes bibliographical references and index. |
Identifiers: LCCN 2024015357 (print) | LCCN 2024015358 (ebook) | ISBN 9781032354750 (hardback) | ISBN 9781032354736 (paperback) | ISBN 9781003327059 (ebook)
Subjects: LCSH: Education, Preschool--Psychological aspects. | Education, Primary--Psychological aspects. | Child psychology. | Child development. | Teacher-student relationships. | Education--Parent participation.
Classification: LCC LB1140.2 .P3658 2025 (print) | LCC LB1140.2 (ebook) | DDC 372.2101/9--dc23/eng/20240521
LC record available at https://lccn.loc.gov/2024015357
LC ebook record available at https://lccn.loc.gov/2024015358

ISBN: 978-1-032-35475-0 (hbk)
ISBN: 978-1-032-35473-6 (pbk)
ISBN: 978-1-003-32705-9 (ebk)

DOI: 10.4324/9781003327059

Typeset in Bembo
by SPi Technologies India Pvt Ltd (Straive)

Contents

Acknowledgements

It is with such great pleasure that I am able to share this series of books with you all. They have been many years in the creating and with numerous people to thank. Firstly, the staff and children at Olney Preschool and Olney Infant Academy in Buckinghamshire, England, the settings of the original research where I shared two years with the most delightful children and wonderfully accommodating and passionate staff.

I would also like to acknowledge the support of Bright Horizons Family Solutions UK, in providing images to illustrate the practice promoted in these publications. The Creative Services team at Bright Horizons worked collaboratively with me to supply the many delightful images of children and their carers engaging in playful and sensitive interactions. The images in these books were captured in various Bright Horizons nurseries throughout England and Scotland and with the kind permission of the parents to use these images of their fabulous children.

And I would like to thank my colleagues and friends at the Centre for Research in Early Childhood in Birmingham, most notably Professor Chris Pascal and Professor Tony Bertram who listened tirelessly to my thoughts and ideas, helping me to unravel my excited sparks of inspiration into well considered observations. A colleague once said to me that true creativity comes from the combination of knowledge, skill, inspiration and persistence all of which were nurtured by this dynamic duo.

But as always, none of this would be possible without the ongoing love and support of my amazing husband and children who never stop believing in me. You have been there to read, to listen and on occasion to add some unique perspectives, all the while keeping me laughing… and fed! I could not do this without you.

Section I
Introduction

Nurturing childhoods for all our tomorrows

Whether you are new to teaching or been in the profession for decades, whether you are an assistant in a classroom of five-year-olds or responsible for schools across a district, you will have your own reasons for reading the books in the Nurturing Childhoods series. But the fact that you are, would suggest that you are well aware of the tremendous impact we all have on all the children in our lives every day, in every plan and decision we make, through every experience we facilitate and interaction we share. In previous books in this series we have looked at what it means to nurture pre-verbal, pre-mobile children, dependent on us for many of their experiences. We have looked at nurturing the expanding world of a toddler as they get to their feet, exploring, interacting and developing a growing sense of all that they are, along with slightly older children, with a few years of experiences influencing the ways in which they engage with their world. Now as our attentions turn to nurturing children through their school years, many of these descriptions will again ring true with experiences very much dependent on the decisions we make, in an expanding world of new opportunities and with thousands of experiences influencing how a child will respond to every one of them.

Throughout this series we have celebrated the fact that children are on a lifelong journey of holistic, interconnected and continuously evolving development. Because of this, many of the themes running through the books are relevant for all children and the intention is that you enjoy them all. For example, I have a chapter in this book called "Understanding Child Anxiety" now that they are experiencing new environments, new experiences and expectations. That does not mean that the developing understanding of their emotions has not been deeply informative already and will continue to be so as their emotional intelligence matures and we will touch on the emotional needs of all children throughout the chapter. A child's need for effective communication,

DOI: 10.4324/9781003327059-1

Nurturing Children's Development	How Can You Help Me to Feel Secure?	How Can You Help Me to Feel Happy?	How Can You Help Me to Learn?	Nurturing GIFTED Learning for Life

NURTURING BABIES	NURTURING TODDLERS	NURTURING CHILDREN THROUGH PRESCHOOL AND RECEPTION	NURTURING THROUGH THE PRIMARY YEARS	
Good Practices from the Start	Understanding Growth in the Toddler Years	Managing the Expectations Placed on Young Children	Developing Reflective Practice and Mindful Development	
Connecting with Babies; Communication, Movement and Play	Connecting with Toddlers; Communication, Movement and Play	Connecting with Young Children; Communication, Movement and Play	Nurturing Engaged School Children; Communication, Movement and Play	
Striking the Right Balance	Time to Get Physical	Helping Young Children Manage Their Emotions in a Social World	Helping Children to feel Safe and Secure	
Time for Rest	Positive Responses to Developing Emotions	Supporting Young Children's Developing Behaviours	Developing Classrooms where Children Think and Express Themselves	Section One
Understanding Babies Responses	Big Emotions and the Behaviours They Can Trigger	Developing Young Children's Confidence to Think and Express Themselves	Understanding Child Anxiety	
Nurturing Babies Developing Behaviours	The Secret to Effective Praise and Encouragement	Nurturing Young Children as they Develop Social Skills	Nurturing Confidence in the Classroom	
Helping Children Feel Competent, Confident and Worthy	Nurturing Toddlers Self-Esteem ~ and Learning How to Keep Hold of It	Understanding Young Children's Friendships	Friendships, Conflict and Playground Dramas	
Empowering Resilient children	Establishing Foundations for a Love of Reading	Understanding the Conflicts of Young Children	Developing Nurturing Methods of Encouragement and Self-motivation	
Supporting Children's Learning	Getting Mathematical	Preparing for School	Supporting Parents to Nurture Their School Child at Home	
Nurturing Lifelong Learning with Babies	Nurturing Lifelong Learning with Toddlers	Supporting Lifelong Learning in the Years Before School	Supporting Lifelong Learning in the Classroom	
The Nurturing Childhoods Pedagogical Framework	The Nurturing Childhoods Pedagogical Framework	The Nurturing Childhoods Pedagogical Framework	The Nurturing Childhoods Pedagogical Framework	
Nurturing Babies to Do Things for Themselves	Nurturing Toddlers to Do Things for Themselves	Nurturing Young Children to Do Things for Themselves	Nurturing School Children to Do Things for Themselves	
Nurturing Babies to Do New Things	Nurturing Toddlers to Do New Things	Nurturing Young Children to Do New Things	Nurturing School Children to Do New Things	
Nurturing Babies to Be Brave	Nurturing Toddlers to Be Brave	Nurturing Young Children to Be Brave	Nurturing School Children to Be brave	Section Two
Nurturing Babies to Have Good Ideas	Nurturing Toddlers to Have Good Ideas	Nurturing Young Children to Have Good Ideas	Nurturing School Children to Have Good Ideas	
Nurturing Babies to Have a Go	Nurturing Toddlers to Have a Go	Nurturing Young Children to Have a Go	Nurturing School Children to Have a Go	
Nurturing Babies to Have Fun	Nurturing Toddlers to Have Fun	Nurturing Young Children to Have Fun	Nurturing School Children to Have Fun	
Nurturing Babies to Think	Nurturing Toddlers to Think	Nurturing Young Children to Think	Nurturing School Children to Think	

Figure S1.1: The four books in this series, exploring the growth and development of children throughout their early childhood and on into the school classroom.

expanding language and sustained play continue to be core themes, even having transitioned to more formal learning environments (Figure S1.1).

When we start talking about nurturing children through their school years, focus can quickly become drawn to the curriculums and frameworks that govern us, the programmes we may be expected to follow and the assessments that keep track of it all. But of course, children and their learning are far more complex than any set of criteria can begin to represent. And we know our children are too important to not look beyond a "one-size-fits-all" curriculum that can change in line with some new directive at any moment. This book is then intended to support you as you reflect on the whole child, not as machines that will produce the desired outcome provided we invest in the right programmes, but as children.

We will look at the opportunities you offer through your teaching, both intrinsically and externally, as you engage children in their experiences of learning. We will look at how this is reflected in how children respond and what this tells us about the deep impact you are having on their dispositions towards learning. I will also introduce you to methods, frameworks and techniques to help illustrate the impact of environmental, social and pedagogical variables on children's experiences as we gain a better understanding of the impact of our pedagogy on each child's developing potential.

When we understand the impact of the experiences we offer children, beyond that offered through traditional methods of testing and assessment, we can gain a critically informed perspective of each child's learning experiences. We can nurture each child's learning journey, mindful of the many influences on their lives, mindful that they are a product of every experience they have ever had and are deeply impacted by the decisions being made on their behalf. And we can show our children the possibilities of learning, we can develop their propensity to think, to be self-aware, confident and unafraid of grappling with and pursuing complex ideas. Because if we don't, the unique potential residing in every child can become devalued, derailed and ultimately we all lose out as they simply disengage. Something you may have already experienced.

Through these books I want you to learn something, but I won't achieve this by simply telling you what I think and expecting you to do the same. Instead, I offer you the knowledge you need to unpick the issues discussed in each chapter, whether this is in the form of learning theories or relevant child development, biological or psychological background. We will then look at the relevance this has before looking at suggestions to support you as you develop your own confident and consistent practice. With every chapter written using the Nurturing Childhoods approach of Knowledge, Understanding and then Support, you will then have all you need to develop practices that are right for you and the children you teach.

Each Section is intended to help you think and reflect, but through their accessible style of writing and illustrations, they can be easily and quickly understood without the need for previous knowledge and are intended to be read and understood by anyone with an interest in how children learn. And because of their foundation in child development (rather than any curriculum, programme or approach), they will always remain relevant, regardless of changes in educational policy or documentation. This is also true whether you are working in the UK, the USA or the UAE; whether you teach in a village, an inner city or a forest; and whatever curriculum or policies guide you, even the decade in which you read these words because nurturing a child's learning is both timeless and universal.

They are also further supported by a setting-based Accreditation and a suite of online courses for parents, practitioners and teachers. You can even join the Nurturing Childhoods Community, share your experiences and receive tons of support and guidance, so for more information head to nurturingchildhoods.com and join me as we start looking beyond our adult agendas and look instead at the children in front of us as together, we develop the potential of all our children.

The learning child... Yes – but what about the rest?

As you will know if you have any experience of children, they tend to have a mind of their own. Their actions are influenced by their choices and their responses are influenced through every experience that has gone before. How well a learning opportunity is responded to is then highly dependent on each child and the realities central to their lives. Trying to plan for a class full of children as if every child's needs are the same is then not only unhelpful, but it also does our children a gross mis-service. And whilst formal classroom pedagogies focusing on the accumulation of discrete skills and knowledge have their place, when this is at the expense of nurturing a child's dispositional engagement or unaware of their sense of security or well-being within the environment, you are going to run into some problems.

Learning involves complex processes of assimilation as children experience, retreat and return to ideas. They are utilising processes that are holistic, continual and episodic, processes that are embedded within the environments we give them access to, the interactions we share and the permissions we offer them to engage. The success of these processes are then reflected in the behaviours and responses being demonstrated, but to see them our focus needs to be on the child in front of us, mindful that they are more than a demonstration of their learning goals.

While you will naturally have curriculum focused agendas throughout the day, when an approach is centred around learning goals and objectives, this provides a structure that our children are expected to fit around when every child is developing at different rates and in different ways. When we focus on one aspect of the multitude of factors influencing how a growing, developing child is learning in this moment, we miss the wide-ranging developments that are occurring and fluctuating over time. And when children who are intrinsically driven to engage with every learning opportunity become limited by demands for specific knowledge and constrained through pre-determined expectations, their love of learning simply wanes as they realise learning... or this environment of learning... simply isn't for them.

As a species, we are hardwired to be curious and increasingly independent, social, self-motivated and courageous. These and other character traits have enabled us to learn and thrive in every climate on the planet for hundreds of thousands of years. We have developed levels of collaboration that have allowed us to establish complex societies. We have employed intuition that lets us know what others may be thinking, using these skills to work towards complex shared goals. And our children are discovering and developing these powerful tools of learning from the moment they are born. This has not changed simply because they have walked into a school classroom and rather than becoming frustrated at the child that needs to have an opinion, to move their body or explore what is going on outside, we need to find ways of embracing these intrinsic methods of learning.

Once a child reaches the school classroom they will have many years' worth of learning experiences behind them. Along with the responses they received when they tried, informing the chance that they will do so again. Now that you are acting as gatekeeper to their learning experiences, you play a tremendous role in how they will learn through every decision, environment and permission you extend. And with every experience informing the next, you are also deeply influencing their ongoing disposition towards their characteristics of learning. Will they develop along positive trajectories as your children become more confident, motivated and curious in the world around them? Or will their experiences see them become timid and more reluctant to engage? How do the experiences you offer stimulate your children or are some learning that this might not be worth their efforts? Are they encouraged to have a thought, an idea or a different response or will only the answer you are thinking of do?

Within a technology rich age, where displays of what is known has become devalued, children need to be comfortable within their abilities to engage in their learning. We need to be nurturing their abilities to solve complex problems within new environments as they produce and combine knowledge rather than simply reproducing it. They need to experience how to manage new problems within unexpected situations, encountering setbacks with motivation and perseverance and exploring alternative directions with courage and insight. Along with the ability to offer opinions, contribute ideas and work collaboratively, unafraid of the requirement for one desired answer.

We must then look beyond learning goals to consider what children need to function within society. And we need to encourage their thinking and actions as they advance beyond responding to the demands of others and repetition of pre-packaged knowledge. When we can set aside the blinkers of curriculum expectations and look too with these deep-rooted processes in mind, we can learn so much more about the journey a child is on. But we need to know what to look for and to understand the difference we make every day to the process.

These books think of children and how we nurture the full scope of their learning and development in a very different way. And it does this by bringing our focus back to the child. Recognising that development is complex, diverse and dependent on many factors and cannot possibly be nurtured until we have explored the wider implications of what it means to be THIS child in THIS moment, who will be greatly influenced by the world around them. We will then look at how you can nurture a child's learning, but we will also look at their holistic development, their happiness and sense of security within the school classroom. To guide you in this, Chapter 10 will then introduce you to GIFTED Learning (the Greater Involvement Facilitated Through Engaging in Dispositions).

We know the importance of a child's well-being and involvement from the work of many esteemed colleagues in the field of education. You may also be familiar with the idea of there being a hierarchy of needs that need addressing. And yet, if we find ourselves overly concerned with development goals, we can lose sight of this and the impact that we ourselves are having. Meaningful learning simply isn't possible if a child does not feel safe and secure in their surroundings. And unless we learn to see children in a more holistic way, the whole set-up is prone to topple. However, many teaching qualifications can lack focus in these areas (Figure S1.2).

In Section 1 you will find chapters looking at how we nurture young children's development, how we help children to feel secure, how we can help them find their happiness and then how we can nurture a growing love of learning and enquiry. All while offering the experiences so important to learning and the development of dispositions common to enthusiastic, lifelong learners.

In Section 2 I will then introduce you to the Nurturing Childhoods Pedagogical Framework (NCPF), aka The Flower along with MICE and TOADs as we explore a new way of thinking about children's learning and the way you observe and facilitate it. Through this range of tools designed to help you understand the learning journey your children are on and to support their engagement in it we recognise the core learning characteristics that are developing in all our children. Recognising the behaviours that demonstrate them and keeping our CHILDREN at the centre of all we do, rather than any external agendas that can change at any moment. Because when we can do that, children flourish in the ways they have been instinctively trying to do for millennia. They can do so as babies, toddlers… and all the way through the school system. In ways that protect them from changing directives, unknown futures and the realities of a universally connected world.

As I have said in previous books, while this may seem a little more complex than a curriculum framework you are familiar with at first, a child's learning is complex. Children are multifaceted, changing minute by minute and vulnerable to any number of influences. They will not demonstrate all they are through an activity planned last week to meet today's learning goals. But they do speak volumes through every behaviour and response, provided you know how to see them. If you want to capture this level of understanding of the children you teach, not only do you need to be mindful of the child in front of you, but you also need methods that will allow for deeper reflection and a more informed awareness of the experiences you offer. Through the Nurturing Childhoods Academy and its suite of resources, you will then have access to all of that too.

Navigating your way around this book

In Section 1 of this book we will look at the importance of reflecting on our teaching practices, mindful of advice and guidance coming from a range of directions and the influences that will ultimately impact the experiences of your children. And we will look at the importance of communication, movement and play in the minds and bodies

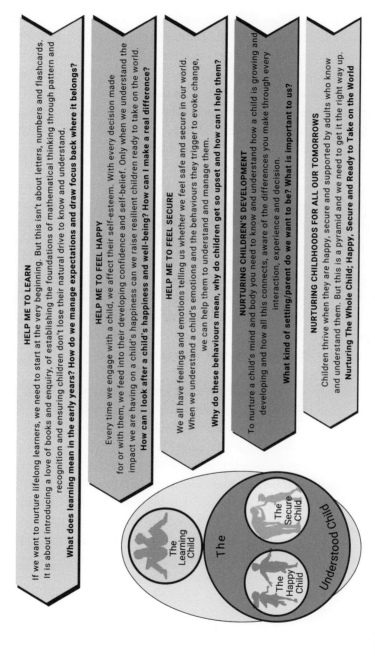

HELP ME TO LEARN

If we want to nurture lifelong learners, we need to start at the very beginning. But this isn't about letters, numbers and flashcards. It is about introducing a love of books and enquiry, of establishing the foundations of mathematical thinking through pattern and recognition and ensuring children don't lose their natural drive to know and understand.

What does learning mean in the early years? How do we manage expectations and draw focus back where it belongs?

HELP ME TO FEEL HAPPY

Every time we engage with a child, we affect their self-esteem. With every decision made for or with them, we feed into their developing confidence and self-belief. Only when we understand the impact we are having on a child's happiness can we raise resilient children ready to take on the world.

How can I look after a child's happiness and well-being? How can I make a real difference?

HELP ME TO FEEL SECURE

We all have feelings and emotions telling us whether we feel safe and secure in our world. When we understand a child's emotions and the behaviours they trigger to evoke change, we can help them to understand and manage them.

Why do these behaviours mean, why do children get so upset and how can I help them?

NURTURING CHILDREN'S DEVELOPMENT

To nurture a child's mind and body you need to know and understand how a child is growing and developing and how all this connects, aware of the differences you make through every interaction, experience and decision.

What kind of setting/parent do we want to be? What is important to us?

NURTURING CHILDHOODS FOR ALL OUR TOMORROWS

Children thrive when they are happy, secure and supported by adults who know and understand them. But this is a pyramid and we need to get it the right way up.

Nurturing The Whole Child; Happy, Secure and Ready to Take on the World

Figure S1.2: Developing the learning skills and capabilities of a child might be at the top of our agenda, but it rests on so much more that we need to get right first.

of children as we nurture dispositions intrinsic to learning and the teaching techniques that continue to engage children in rich, diverse learning experiences (Figure S1.3).

As we look at helping children to feel safe and secure within our environments we will look at ways of nurturing the developing emotions and behaviours of children within the school classroom as we look to understand how a child's emotions can feel, how difficult they can be to express and the fallout that might be experienced. And we will look at ways we can develop our classrooms into spaces where children are encouraged to think and express themselves, to have the skills to see, hear and understand a situation and to reach their own conclusions with unique insight and ideas.

As we look at helping young children to feel happy, we will explore where child anxiety can come from, how to recognise it and steps you can take to help children with feelings and emotions they may be struggling to manage. And we will look at ways of nurturing their coping skills and confidence, in the classroom and out of it. While at the same time, being aware of the warning signs that something may be troubling them at levels they can no longer manage without support. And we will look at friendship dilemmas, disputes and how to recognise when these might need a level of adult intervention.

And as we look at helping young children to learn, we will look at supporting children as they take more ownership of their goals, intentions and outcomes, how we can encourage children to feel motivated and the subtle changes of approach that make all the difference. We will look at the importance of homework and how parents can encourage their child's learning without damaging their desire to do it. And we will look at the impact of a child's learning experiences on their future dispositions towards learning, understanding the importance of offering children GIFTED Learning and how this can enhance your teaching.

As I have said throughout the books in this series, children need to feel happy and secure before they can settle into any higher order activities. They are developing in response to all the opportunities that surround them. And they have minds and bodies growing through the same mechanisms and processes that have ensured our survival as a species for hundreds of thousands of years. But to nurture this in our children means placing THEM at the centre of all we do. In Section II we will then look at the Nurturing Childhoods Pedagogical Framework (NCPF), the ABCs of Developing Engagement (ABCoDE) and the OPTED Scale. And to support you as you consider the multiple variables of teaching styles, engagements and class groupings you have available to you I will introduce you to MICE and TOADs as you recognise the impact of previous experiences on your children's dispositional engagements and develop methods of enhancing them.

Then in the final chapters, we will look at what our young children are communicating to us through their evolving behaviours and the powerful ways we have to nurture their development through some key practices. With the help of the NCPF, the ABCoDE and the OPTED Scale and with MICE and TOADs to advise and guide, we can then re-evaluate the teaching styles our children experience and the opportunities these offer for them to think, to try, to do and have fun.

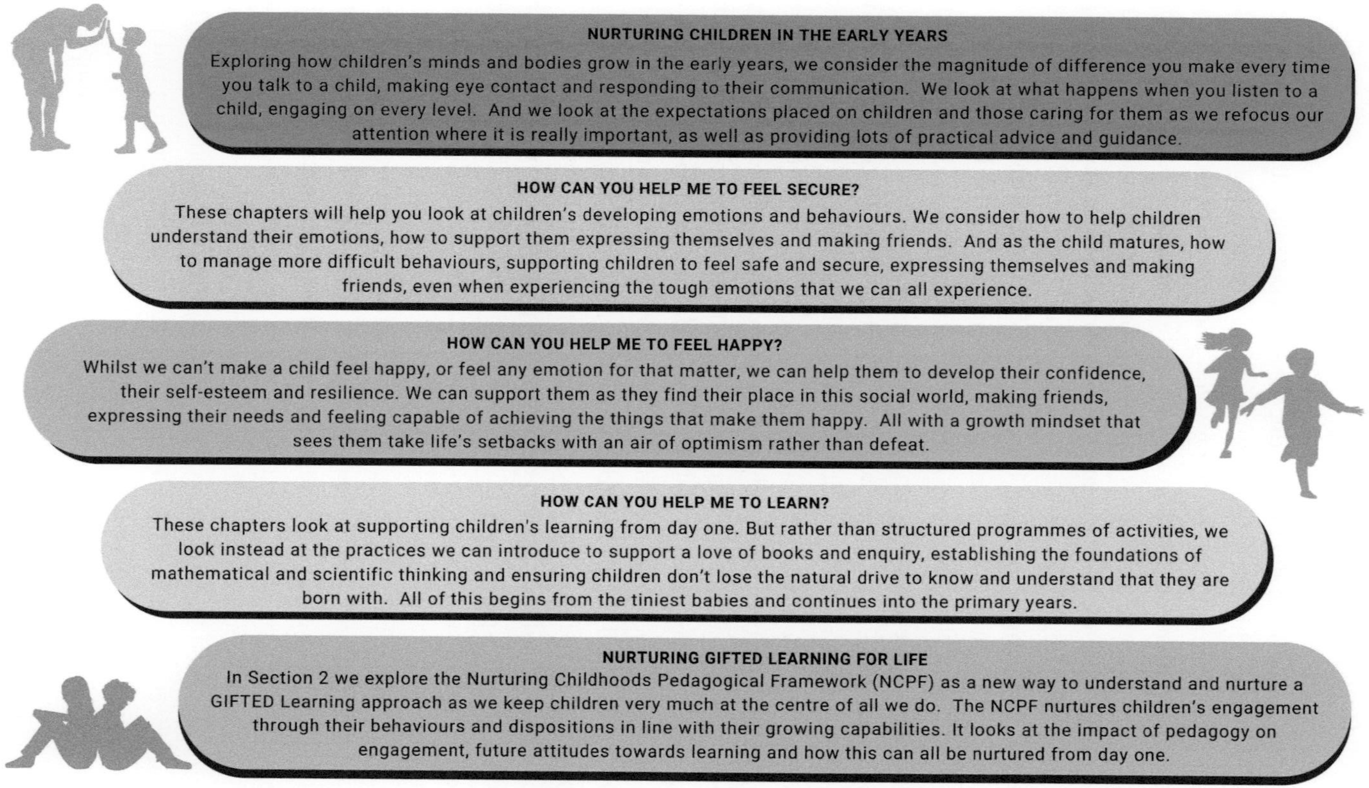

NURTURING CHILDREN IN THE EARLY YEARS

Exploring how children's minds and bodies grow in the early years, we consider the magnitude of difference you make every time you talk to a child, making eye contact and responding to their communication. We look at what happens when you listen to a child, engaging on every level. And we look at the expectations placed on children and those caring for them as we refocus our attention where it is really important, as well as providing lots of practical advice and guidance.

HOW CAN YOU HELP ME TO FEEL SECURE?

These chapters will help you look at children's developing emotions and behaviours. We consider how to help children understand their emotions, how to support them expressing themselves and making friends. And as the child matures, how to manage more difficult behaviours, supporting children to feel safe and secure, expressing themselves and making friends, even when experiencing the tough emotions that we can all experience.

HOW CAN YOU HELP ME TO FEEL HAPPY?

Whilst we can't make a child feel happy, or feel any emotion for that matter, we can help them to develop their confidence, their self-esteem and resilience. We can support them as they find their place in this social world, making friends, expressing their needs and feeling capable of achieving the things that make them happy. All with a growth mindset that sees them take life's setbacks with an air of optimism rather than defeat.

HOW CAN YOU HELP ME TO LEARN?

These chapters look at supporting children's learning from day one. But rather than structured programmes of activities, we look instead at the practices we can introduce to support a love of books and enquiry, establishing the foundations of mathematical and scientific thinking and ensuring children don't lose the natural drive to know and understand that they are born with. All of this begins from the tiniest babies and continues into the primary years.

NURTURING GIFTED LEARNING FOR LIFE

In Section 2 we explore the Nurturing Childhoods Pedagogical Framework (NCPF) as a new way to understand and nurture a GIFTED Learning approach as we keep children very much at the centre of all we do. The NCPF nurtures children's engagement through their behaviours and dispositions in line with their growing capabilities. It looks at the impact of pedagogy on engagement, future attitudes towards learning and how this can all be nurtured from day one.

Figure S1.3: Through these chapters we will explore the importance of nurturing children holistically throughout their early childhood and the primary years.

Igniting the potential of dispositional development

This book is underpinned by a longitudinal study that looked to capture children's responses to formal learning environments. Concerned that children's natural propensities for learning can become disengaged once overly academic objectives direct their experiences of learning, this phenomenological study explored the effects on children through a range of environments, teaching styles and interactions, noting how their engagement across a range of dispositions were being impacted. Observing different environments, permissions, expectations and social groupings this study offered a unique insight into children's responses to learning. As opportunities for dispositional engagement changed and children's experiences became more constrained, children who had been observed as enthusiastic, engaged learners in their previous settings were seen to become reluctant and reticent in their new environments. And as their identities were taking shape within the classroom, the deeper life-skills and characteristics underpinning them became a real cause for concern.

We know learning does not occur within a vacuum, that it is situated within the moment and impacted through a multitude of variables unique to the learner and the instant in which it was captured. We also know that a child's opportunities will understandably be driven and governed by adults throughout much of their day. However, if the perception of a valuable experience is only derived from meeting an external agenda, lesson objective or attained skill, many foundational experiences will be overlooked. For example, if we want our children to remain motivated in their pursuit of a difficult or long-term goal, they need to have experienced being courageous, continuing with something in the hope of success and secure in their eventual ability to succeed. If you want a child to manage the complex processes involved in solving an equation, structuring the paragraphs of their writing or thinking through the steps of an experiment, they need to have imagination with the curiosity and adaptability required to use it.

But this comes from giving children a voice, a choice and opportunities to think for themselves, whilst retaining their innate behaviours, their natural inquisitiveness and harnessing their desires to engage. Because if we fail to do so, we significantly limit their academic potential with knock on effects throughout their emotional and social development. However, this requires definitions of teaching and learning that look further than discrete or adult led learning goals, teaching objectives or produced data. It calls for teaching practices that advocate for a child's right to think, to question and imagine as they demonstrate their capabilities to themselves as much as others.

Whilst sitting alongside any curriculum, MICE and TOADs offer a comprehensive and holistic lens through which you can capture, not only the messy constructs residing within learning and development, but also the social and cultural realities of children within their experiences of learning. By consciously removing its focus from the desired learning outcomes, MICE and TOADs look to acknowledge and recognise the impact of pedagogy, formal and otherwise, on the engagements of children, both in the moment and as predispositions take root. Recognising the direct impact that pedagogical choices have on children's depth of engagement, their attitudes towards their learning and the outcomes being achieved.

With school readiness agendas focusing too frequently on children's ability to conform to the requirements of the classroom, if we are to realise every child's true potential, could it be the expectations of the classroom that need reforming? Imagine if a dispositional focus rooted in the theories and methods offered here were to accompany widely scrutinised performance criteria and publicised achievements. Think what could be possible if children's natural instincts for learning were being harnessed, nurtured and acknowledged, celebrating all children's full potential, wherever it may reside. As you look to offer your children the most enriched teaching experiences, I hope this book helps you to actively consider how your children engage and connect with the processes of learning. Harnessing these most basic of natural human instincts that have allowed us all to achieve staggering levels of learning since our first days of life.

Developing reflective practice and mindful development

How you planned to teach and nurture the developing mind and body of a child may not have been something you gave particularly serious thought to before you embarked upon it. Beyond that is, vowing to do it differently to your own experiences, to emulate a particular theory or to never make a child do that thing you always hated in school. However, once we are faced with the reality of teaching children, we can find ourselves needing to make important decisions every day. Often very quickly and potentially when we are not in the best place to do so. Tired, stressed, pushed for time or resources or simply the peace and quiet to stop and think. And in these conditions, it can become all too easy to fall into familiar patterns.

Ultimately, the decisions you make for a child and the teaching practices you choose to follow are all yours. Even if you are teaching in what seems to be a heavily regulated environment. The way you engage with children and the opportunities you give them in this moment are down to you. And these will originate from a mix of your training and your past experiences, scientific research, anecdotal advice, family truisms and, let's face it, what seems right at the time. Whatever direction you do choose to take, your children need you to follow it with consistency and confidence. But how do you go about taking advice and making changes secure in the knowledge that it is the best thing to be doing?

There are certainly many places you may turn to for trusted, knowledgeable advice. Some of which will fill you with the faith that you are doing what is best for the children in your life. Others will leave you feeling unsure and anxious, questioning the validity of what you are hearing. And yet childhood is too important a period of time to blindly embrace techniques that are being advocated by others without firstly considering the rationale or science behind them. Research into childhood development, growth and learning has also taken massive strides forward. So, whilst I will be the first to advocate many approaches of years gone by, that does not mean you should do something in a certain way simply because that is how it has always been done. Nor because that is what everyone else seems to be doing.

DOI: 10.4324/9781003327059-2

Knowledge

Know the importance of reflecting on practice, mindful of the impact teaching styles have on children's experiences

When it comes to teaching, you may have heard of or be familiar with many styles, techniques and theories. Some of which may be echoes from your own childhood or a repeat of what you see and hear around you. Others may involve different teaching styles or learning theories than you were used to. They may suggest unusual approaches or responses towards children, that are spoken of with great reverence, promising guaranteed success and easy outcomes. Some of which may seem like a great idea, others may sit uncomfortably from the start. But hey, those promised outcomes are pretty alluring! (Figure 1.1)

Figure 1.1: In a busy classroom it is easy to fall into familiar teaching styles and practices without really examining the processes occurring or how this is experienced by each child.

You may then find yourself doing things in a certain way because you think you should. But where do these messages come from? Do you find yourself repeating phrases or practices that you swore you never would? Or going through the day without really thinking about why you are doing something in a particular way? It is not until we pause for a moment, listen and actively consider what we are doing that we can become aware of the affects we are having on children. So, as you read this book, take the time to reflect and enjoy the journey of learning as it helps you grow and discover alongside the children in your life.

Reflect on the practices worth following

No matter how long you have been around children, being offered advice is something you will be remarkably familiar with. You will be introduced to lots of tools and sure-fire methods, some of which, in the short-term, may seem to be working. But no matter how much experience you have, it is hugely important that you consider and question any advice you are given. To make any decision based on the anecdotal stories of others is, unsurprisingly, known as reasoning by anecdote. But without further evidence to back an anecdote up, it is not much better than simply guessing. And without processes of structured reflection, ineffectual methods may be wholeheartedly embraced without question.

As you cast a reflective eye on the activities being offered to children be particularly wary of all the "must have" development-promoting programmes suggesting that they will make a child more intelligent, be quicker to develop or astound with results. There is little evidence that these have any long-term impact, or even work in the short term, as many costly lawsuits can lay testament. What they can do however is take a child away from the really important foundational work of childhood that can be well supported within any environment. Provided we learn to look at the child in front of us, we are aware of the dispositions of lifelong learning that are establishing and we continue to offer lots of opportunities to play.

It is then so important that before we embrace any new technique, that we reflect on our knowledge of child development, mindful of its long-term impact. Take a moment and consider whether you like the way others are doing something or are you following simply because that is how it has always been done. Learn to see ready-made, pre-packaged solutions for what they are before they backfire or see you make a costly mistake. And no matter how much something is being advocated or endorsed, scratch the surface to look closely at the methods being used. If these go against your understanding of how a child learns or their need to feel confident and empowered, safe and secure, ask yourself "At what cost?" Because, only when you become accustomed to doing this can you begin to separate what is right for you and your children. And what is not.

The impact of your interactions

When you engage with a child, assuming you are looking to do this with consistency, your chosen style is going to become a familiar experience. Feeding into and influencing their experiences and how they then respond to them. Your approach needs to be well-considered and grounded in some basic understanding of how children develop, in their mind and body, as well as with regard to their emotional stability and core capabilities. So, as you influence their deep-rooted growth and development every day, be mindful of the impact of your actions, no matter how automatic they may become.

Consider…

- The ways in which you interact
- How you set them a task
- The expectations you place on them
- The limits you place on their use of the environment and its resources
- The engagements that are permitted with their peers
- How you respond to their behaviours
- And how you manage your own.

Any practices you follow are doing so much more than managing a child's behaviours and responses in the moment, they are moulding all their future behaviours.

They are also setting their understanding and expectations of themselves and of how the world works. And they are building and reinforcing the relationship they have with you.

So, when you find crayons thrown all over the floor, stop for a moment and hear the difference between "Look what you've done!" and the alternative message of empowerment that could be used "You can fix the mess you made, I know you can". Or when your question to the group is met with an unexpected answer, how different "No, does anyone else know?" sounds, compared to "That's interesting, why do you think that?" While one approach can have a child surrounded by negativity or put downs, convinced they are not good enough, another can give them ownership of their thoughts and actions, even the undesired ones.

The impact of your approach

As you consider the style of your approach, you may prefer a heavily structured environment with clear expectations and guidelines to be followed. Alternatively, you may look to offer children more freedoms, where they can direct their own learning. While children learn well within a range of classrooms and environments, be careful of having too much of a good thing.

Within an overly structured environment children may experience more "control" than guidance. Frequently met with a "Because I said so" mentality, this limits their opportunity to seek out knowledge, to make the connections they need or to experience a sense of personal ownership. Nor does it invite questions or opportunities to explore their understanding, to explain their reasoning or uncover deeper thoughts or misconceptions. Within a strict or highly controlling environment, children may appear to be very well behaved. But this may be coming from a place of fear; fear of negative attention or fear of what it means to step outside of the rules. And whilst it might seem to be results driven, it is not embedding the experiences or abilities conducive to future learning, problem solving or understanding.

Too little structure and the teaching experience can feel chaotic or lacking in control. Within an environment that lacks any form of clear, positive message, a child may feel that you are not overly interested in their behaviours. They may be unclear of what to expect or what the expectations are on them. Within either of these environments, emotions can typically run deep as both adults and children struggle to understand what to expect. Hard lines one day may be followed by second chances the next. Bribes or veiled threats may be used to control access to play, but without the necessary structure to carry this through. In this environment, children are unlikely to feel secure and may begin to view themselves and the world around them with a lack of confidence.

When you offer children a degree of autonomy in their learning experiences, they have the scope to find the engagement and opportunities required for making deep connections in their learning. Together with supervised experiences of finding their own way, children can learn from their mistakes through the freedoms they are given to make them. Responsive to their immediate needs, you can be quick to nurture, communicate and talk about what they are doing as you guide, structure and explain (Figure 1.2).

Within a warm, guided environment you can ensure clear limits are in place and enforced. Yet at the same time, see that children are listened to, that their thoughts and ideas are heard and explored and they are invited to express their wishes and needs in the moment. Children can then be encouraged to think

Figure 1.2: When we talk to children about their ideas and really listen to their thought processes we can understand how their thinking is developing, the connections they are making and understand any misconceptions.

for themselves and participate in the decisions that are made. Whilst strict procedures and lesson plans will on occasion need to be followed, in this learning environment, the adults are keen to explain why. Balancing strong mature control with warmth and communication. All of which needs grounding in a knowledge of children's development, their prior experiences and the expectations you can place on their behaviours.

Understanding

Understand the positive and negative impact of your practice on children, as you learn to consider their needs with fresh eyes

On hearing these descriptions of teaching approaches, you may not consider yourself to fit into any definition in its extreme. You may fall more broadly into one style, in the middle of a couple or find that it depends on the situation. You might find yourself using different approaches at different times of the day or for different purposes. But it is important to note that the styles you are using will inform the relationship you have with your children and the ways in which they behave and develop. It will have an impact on their state of mind, their approach to learning and their ways of thinking. While also being deeply impactful on their emotional well-being. So, as you reflect on your teaching decisions, your interactions and permissions, do so mindfully and with conviction and consistency.

Understanding your style

Children, no matter their age or the issues they are facing, need to feel safe and secure in your care. And the quickest way you will undermine this is for them to not have faith in the decisions you are making. Like with anything, if you want to employ a consistent approach, you need to have some form of structure behind your thinking. Even if you do not know what your approach is called or are even fully aware that it is occurring. Imagine a remodel of your home before deciding on the style you are trying to achieve or planning the menu of an important meal before deciding on whether you are serving a buffet breakfast or formal supper.

Rules are an important part of this process and should be embraced as a positive and important part of guiding children's growth and development. We all have to live by rules in our life; in sport they provide the purpose, structure and directions for the game being played; in society rules look to create an ideal environment for people to coexist in peace. Far from constraining, they keep us safe, keep our games fair and offer expected consequences for when the rules are broken.

Without rules or direction within their physical or emotional environment children can become disoriented and confused, losing sight of who they are or what they can achieve. And in the absence of any guidance children can begin to feel lost, seeking comfort, support or recognition from anyone willing to offer it. When you offer active guidance children are shown behaviours to model. Within a dependable structure, they experience the sense of security necessary to learn through their responses to situations. Together with the opportunities they need to grow. And when a child's contributions, ideas and opinions are acknowledged and respected within this process they can become confident in expressing themselves, expressing their own instincts and considering them worthy. So, it is worth pausing for a moment to consider the nature of your structures, styles and boundaries from a child's perspective by considering the long-term impact you are having on them.

Understand the need for structure

Children need structure and guidance. They need a stable environment in which to grow, that is both flexible and adaptable to circumstance whilst offering boundaries that allow them to explore their choices. Boundaries and appropriate discipline are important and amongst the most loving things you can offer a child as you seek to teach and guide them. Provided these lessons come from a place of respect, knowledge and awareness and the child is coming from a place of secure emotional well-being. They will then look to you to offer this guidance and structure. They do not need you to be their best friend, they have plenty of those, your role is to teach and guide them as they learn how to be healthy, happy and strong. When this is provided with open compassion, children are provided with the opportunity to thrive, emotionally, physically and morally as well as academically.

When consistent behaviours, structure and fairness are experienced, children learn to find their place in the world. They learn that they can have an opinion, that they can say no and be listened to. The adult is still very much in charge, setting the ground rules but they are happy to discuss these rules. Even if the child does not fully understand, taking the time to have these discussions makes all the difference as reasons are offered and limits considered within warm, trusting relationships. And as the child gains this greater understanding of the rules, they are more likely to follow them.

Understand the effects of too much structure

That said, if you seek to confine a child's day within a carefully planned structure, you seek to eliminate choice. If children are used to being told what to do, they are lost when having to think for themselves. If they are not taught how to think about a situation themselves, they are not learning how to critically reflect on the issues involved. If their ideas or responses are being ignored, overridden or undervalued, they are being taught what to think, not how to think. And if they learn to become easily manipulated into what others are telling them, they may do so at the expense of what is right for themselves. When a child becomes accustomed to doing what they are expected to do next without question, you are reducing their need to be self-motivated or self-regulated. This might sound like an advantage in a busy school classroom but when you ask yourself what characteristics you would want for your children when they go out alone in the world, you may arrive at a different conclusion.

Children who become used to heavily structured environments often experience negative effects on their self-esteem and social skills. They tend to be more rigid in their thinking, perform less well at creative or problem-solving tasks and have less well-developed self-regulation and executive functioning skills. Remember, you are not looking to develop the perfect "school child" but a thinking, autonomous and capable individual without the need for constant, heavy regulation.

Understanding an environment of autonomous learning

As children develop, they begin by obeying and responding to the influences around them. Behaving as they are told to in the moment. They then learn to conform with others and follow the rules, behaving as others are. After this comes a more mature process as children behave in ways that they perceive as being right or wrong, behaving as they think they should. As you guide children through this process, they need structure and rules in order to feel safe and secure. But these need to be carefully thought through and established (Figure 1.3).

Research shows that children experiencing disciplined structures that allow for reasoning are more aware of how decisions affect others and are then better at managing their own conflicts with peers. When taught respect, rather than having it demanded of them, children learn to listen, to be respectful and to expect to be respected themselves. When their independence is celebrated, they develop a sense of themselves, and the communities they live in, learning compassion and to be compassionate toward others. Through empathy and love children find a sense of their own power, rather than having the power of others thrust upon them or seeking to control others. And within environments of love, acceptance and encouragement children recognise their own sense of self and value.

Figure 1.3: Establishing a classroom environment that is both safe and secure while offering provocations that encourage children to think and explore, both inside and out, establishes a sense of autonomy in their learning processes.

Support

Be supported to evaluate current practice and new initiatives, armed with the tools to challenge when something is not right for your children

When employing a structure to your teaching style, philosophies or pedagogy it is important that you take the time to understand a child's development as you evaluate the methods you may be considering. That may sound obvious, but external agendas will often get in the way of this if we do not make the conscious effort to step back and think about the practices we are routinely following. When you take time to reflect on your teaching with open eyes, the impact you are having on a child can be seen with greater clarity. Provided you focus on the child, leaving all other distractions and agendas to one side and are open to the changes you can make.

- How is a child's mind and body developing at this moment?

- What are reasonable expectations?

- Whose agenda are you following?

■ What are their developmental priorities?

■ Not just in terms of this year's goals but in the development of a lifelong learner.

Reflecting on practice

We have all been parented and taught during our childhood, whoever that was by or the style that was used. Regardless of how these experiences affected you or your intentions, you have probably observed familiar patterns within your own practice. Possibly even modelled in the behaviours of your children. But it is only when we stop for a moment and listen to ourselves that we can reflect on our practice and ask ourselves if this is what we want for our children. Of course, to really understand the style of your practice and the effect this is having, you could talk to your children. Ask them about the decisions, rules and guidelines that are being used. And talk to them about the behaviours they demonstrate as you invite them to think about what they are doing and why.

Studies show that the style of engagements children are surrounded by strongly correlates with the way in which they develop and the level of their wellbeing. And this is as true for you as it is your children. So, avoid seeking to manage your children and instead allow them to inspire you. See their tireless efforts to master something they are genuinely interested in, their optimistic joy at every new discovery and their fascination with a new experience. Look to reconnect with the beauty and simplicity of learning in the moment, remembering a time when the anxieties of your adult role were less of a concern.

Whatever you choose to do, whatever approaches you take, these need to be grounded in an understanding of how your children are developing in their mind and in their body. Along with how their cognitive abilities are maturing. And when a practice is recommended, stop for a moment and consider more than the headlines and dig a little deeper. Look at its effects through a more informative lens as you start to recognise the impact of every day on a child's long-term outcomes.

Know your children

To be in the best position to make decisions for the children in your care, you need to be in tune with their developmental stage, their needs, their current frame of mind and how all of this fits into the class as a whole. While this might sound like a tall order within your busy day, look at all the things you are doing and consider honestly which of them are needed. Are large group sessions always the best way? For every child? If you are finding yourself frazzled during "pinch-points" of the day, could there be a reason why?

To support a child, you need to stay well-informed and involved with them, establishing a good relationship from the beginning. This comes from being present in their lives, welcoming to their thoughts and ideas and vigilant of any changes. The most successful way to then promote their learning is for them to see how much you value the learning experiences they are having. This means engaging with them in genuine ways as you look to understand their thought processes, rather than simply eliciting the expected response.

When you do offer your unhurried and focused time to explore what they are thinking, they can experience the power of what they can do for themselves. And as you

Figure 1.4: Engaging with children and sharing in the moment of learning has deeper impact on the processes of understanding than another instruction.

spend quality time interacting, you let them know they are valued, by you and as a member of the group. So, actively schedule in times when this level of engagement is possible. The activity does not have to be structured or involve any pre-planned objective, timings can change and how you engage with each child will be markedly different, but for a few moments, forget other distractions and connect with each child on their level (Figure 1.4).

You are then better able to consider the approaches that are right for them and for the group as you re-evaluate your expectations. You can reflect on how your teaching style fits with their abilities to understand and manage, in mind and body and how your methods fit into the group as a whole. When you then consider your long-term aspirations for your children, think of the attitudes, beliefs and characteristics you would choose for them to grow up with. What behaviours are you looking to nurture? All these questions will help you to take any advice you hear in a more informed way as you decide what is right for you and your children. Regardless of who said it, who is doing it or what kind of thinking is apparently behind it.

Know your practice

We have all been there. Seduced by programs, resources or devices that promise to offer you ways to "supercharge" your children's development. Even if you could find something that genuinely supported accelerated learning, if you seek to rush in one area, fundamental developments will be overlooked in others. How many "gifted" adults do you know of who struggle in social situations? A fantastic aptitude for maths or music should be celebrated and explored, but no one thing should dominate during this time of core development. There are very good reasons why children take all of their childhood to develop. They have been doing a marvellous job of getting it just right for many more years than we have been studying to understand the processes involved. Often the best thing we can do is get out of the way and let them do what they are naturally evolved to want to do.

Other times a child will need the right guidance and support to navigate all the demands and distractions of modern life while learning all they need to about it. Children today are living in a vastly different world to the one you grew up in. In addition to all the challenges of growing up, they are also facing issues that we may struggle at times to understand. Now more than ever, you cannot afford to be complacent, assuming that they have everything under control simply because they tell you they do or because they are not saying otherwise. Ensure your children are given a voice and the understanding they need to use it.

When you are looking to make a change, do then get your children involved when you can. This way they will feel more empowered and more likely to commit to the changes. Not to mention the direct impact this is likely to have on their wellbeing. As well as teaching them techniques to address the current problem you are facing, you can also teach children how to systematically explore alternative methods and actions. During this process they can learn to take responsibility as they try different approaches and become adaptable ready for when future problems arise.

When you are looking to evaluate your practice or make a change it can be useful to keep an honest and careful journal of the changes you are making and the impact you are having. Becoming a "practitioner-scientist" in this way can help you in taking an evidence-based approach to your practice. Using systematic approaches to record these changes will make this process more visible and therefore manageable. It can also help you mentally and practically to get through some difficult challenges. Often the changes we make can be slight or feel like they are going in the wrong direction until you look back at how things were a couple of weeks ago. Alternatively, an improvement in the beginning could have plateaued or even now be making things worse. Viewing the changes made over a longer period will help you to see things clearly.

And when you are given advice... ask yourself, am I really being told the whole story? Their children may be reciting all their multiplication tables, but at what cost? Do you really need to purchase this expensive solution or would its manufacturer just really like you to? And is the advice based on clear, rational logic or fear. Fear of keeping up, fear of not achieving unrealistic goals or matching unachievable demands? Try if you can to not become swayed by what everyone else is doing. If it does not feel right to you, then it is not right for you, possibly for reasons you do not understand beyond your gut-instinct. And have these conversations with whoever you need to. If you do not advocate for the experiences your children really need, who will?

2 Nurturing engaged school children

Communication, movement and play

Very young children the world over are bursting with the need to know, to understand and to investigate, fuelled by dispositions that are hardwired into us before we are born. You will recognise this in the rapid rate of learning and development that occurs during the first years of life. When children start school, some of the freedoms that had been experienced during the early years can become more limited, affecting children's access to these dispositions. And children, once bursting with the need to learn and investigate, can seem to disengage. Whether this is a symptom of a premature start, incompatible techniques or constraining environments, the start of school can be a struggle for many children who still need to move freely, communicate and play.

As parents, carers and educators, we want to give our children every chance to develop in the best ways they can. And there are many programmes promising accelerated learning techniques that may seem to offer this. But wanting children to develop faster is not the same as wanting children to develop well. While focus in the classroom may become more directed towards academic demands, such as maths or reading, a child's methods of learning are no different than they have been before. They need to be interested, they need opportunity to engage and they need to communicate, to move and to play. For these reasons and many others, when it comes to a child's development and learning, faster is not better. In fact, faster can be much worse. Children need to accomplish a great deal in such a short space of time, but these things take time as they lay the foundations for all the learning to come.

When we give children opportunities to learn new skills with an element of play, they find something that they enjoy and are more likely to connect, engaging with the activity for the time they need to benefit from it. Within the freedoms of playful learning children can explore complex concepts without fear of mistakes or the limits of there being one right response. And they can find their voice, as they develop different ways of understanding and expressing what they know. Engaging in mind and body in ways that continue to be essential for life. In fact, if you take a look at the last thing you enjoyed

DOI: 10.4324/9781003327059-3

learning as an adult, you will probably find elements of "playing with ideas", "having a go" and "seeing what you can do". Whether this was learning a foreign language ready for a trip, understanding how to take the perfect picture or decorating a cake.

However, these learning techniques, important to us all, can become somewhat overlooked in a classroom. As important as they are to any form of learning, children have not yet amassed the bank of experiences that you may rely on and their need to embrace learning processes throughout their whole body is felt even deeper. Children need to repeat, reflect and go back to a concept, trying it in different contexts with a different question in their mind as they make connections within their learning. They need to engage in different learning styles and activities as they see what they are doing, its impact and its relevance. And they need to talk about what they are doing, learning from each other as they establish their identity as a confident learner. It is no wonder then that communication, movement and play are commonly recognised as the foundation and most important work of childhood.

Knowledge

Know the importance of communication, movement and play in the minds and bodies of children in the classroom

As you look to manage schedules full of demands, remember that what your children really need from you is to schedule the time they need to become fully engaged with the opportunities for learning you are surrounding them with. They need to be creative, with time to relax and ponder. They need opportunities to explore and interact with other children and the environment during free, unstructured play. And they need to spread their wings as an inquisitive learner as they understand the potential of what this means. This may take more planning than you think when hours of the day can already feel heavily scheduled. However, with some slight tweaks in your approaches, you can make a big difference. And the opportunities you give children for acquiring essential learning dispositions will make this a worthwhile effort. Especially during their early experiences of your classroom as you set in motion the experiences of learning that all others will be based upon.

Communication

Research shows that in today's busy, technology-saturated world, many children are finding their opportunities for the natural forms of playful learning that were once relied upon to have become increasingly limited. Children now spend half as much time playing outside as their parents did, and whilst this is evidently having an impact on their general level of physical fitness, it is also affecting much that we cannot see. As well as many health-related concerns, children's minds and bodies are not gaining the physical experiences or social interactions they require, with impacts felt on their mental health and well-being, as well as their ability to communicate and form friendships. If more social experiences of play have been limited during their early years, children are likely to arrive at school with poor communication skills and their verbal methods of learning and understanding are going to be at risk.

Whilst two-way communication will be a core method of teaching and expressing understanding, for many children this may present a struggle. As screens have become inevitable from younger and younger ages, for some this has replaced much of the physical play synonymous with childhood. As I have explored throughout this series of books, this is bad news for our children's development on many levels, but especially on their developing methods of communication. Children need expressive two-way conversation to develop the communication skills they need. They require responsive experiences of varied interactions as they develop their muscle memory, tone and control. Along with experiencing increasingly complex social interactions with their peers as the social customs and practices of good communication are rehearsed. A screen is doing none of this (Figure 2.1).

Figure 2.1: How will we manage this task? Children need opportunities to talk through their ideas, to be listened to and to hear the ideas of others.

A child's mental state is affected very much in the present, so while a child may find screens fun and entertaining, even small amounts of time on them can have the potential to measurably impact their mental function and executive control. Studies have shown reductions in children's problem-solving abilities after just nine minutes of viewing, affecting their ability to independently focus their attention and resist distraction. This is impacting children's mental flexibility and their self-control, with obvious impact on their school performance, social skills and behaviours that can appear months and even years later. As well as doing little to stimulate interactive communication or even eye contact. So, if you are struggling with a child's communication skills, their exposure to screen time may well be an area to consider.

Today, screen and gaming opportunities surround our children. While some can offer positive effects on their perceptual and cognitive development, creativity and self-esteem, others are consistently associated with poorer achievement in school. As peer influence becomes more pronounced, children may find themselves accessing screens most evenings, on the weekends and any other chance they get. So, when you consider the opportunities you have during the day for two-way communication, the old-fashioned way, be sure to encourage your children to use their words, to engage socially, have an opinion and find their voice.

Movement

Physical development is a core element of the growth our young children undertake throughout the early years of life and represent a significant part of their readiness for school. And yet studies using research methods such as the Movement Assessment Battery for Children (Movement ABC-2) repeatedly show that our children's physical development on entry to the school classroom is significantly behind where it was a decade ago. In some of these studies, around 30% of the children have scored below the 16th percentile, enough to identify them as being at risk of or as having a movement difficulty. Suggesting that the movement opportunities our children receive during early childhood are not sufficient to prepare them for the demands of life.

Children starting, and then leaving their first year of schooling with levels of physical development below where they should be is a growing concern. This is seen in movement difficulties, particularly within fine motor skills and reflected in children's handwriting and poor pencil grip. With studies such as the Big Moves project indicating that many children have been unable to complete the basic physical skills and movement patterns designed for baseline testing.

Children are experiencing

■ Less coordination and poor proprioception

■ Clumsiness and being unaware of personal space

■ Slouching rather than sitting upright

■ Poor gross motor control; skipping, hopping, jumping, balancing and ball control

■ Poor fine motor control; pencil and tool control

■ Lack of muscle tone and mobility

■ Poor core body strength and stability

■ Quick to tire with complaints of aching

■ Lack of stamina

■ Lack of perseverance

In some schools, intervention programmes are being used to address the physical development needs of young children. With the aim of improving both their fine and gross motor skills, children are given exercises designed to revisit key stages in their physical development such as rolling, crawling "commando style" and rocking on all fours. However, for many children, basic skills such as balancing on one leg, holding an "on all fours" position, crawling and marching are proving to be problematic. With these movements specifically chosen to demonstrate a child's physical ability across their developmental milestones, this is a real worry. Suggesting underlying issues within their postural stability, head control, balance, body awareness and the coordination of their limbs. So, if your children are showing a reluctance to sit still, it is probably because their bodies are desperate for the movement it still needs.

Play

Play is the foundation and most important work of childhood. Yet within many children's experiences of childhood there are increasingly less opportunities for traditional forms of play than children had a generation or two ago. With deep rooted impact on their physical, mental and social development play must be viewed with greater insight than a break between the real work or a chance to blow off steam.

From the time they are born, children are learning through their play. As they grow and develop, the ways in which they play will change from "observer play," as they watch other children playing, to "parallel play," at around three-years old as they mirror other children's actions more closely. By around four-years old, children will have begun to engage in "associative play" as they begin acting out short, simple scenarios with others, playing house or going to the market. This stage of play sees children playing in the same space and often with the same games or toys, although there does not tend to be much coordinated interaction. This comes with "cooperative play" as the pretend play becomes fully interactive, seeing children act out increasingly elaborate and prolonged scenes with their peers.

At this stage children will begin to engage in increasingly complex games that involve elements of pretending. This "sociodramatic play" may seem somewhat whimsical but is in fact quite a mentally engaging task. Within it, children are developing dual representation, where they can "be" more than one person or where an object can be more than one thing, even multiple

Figure 2.2: In play we can take on all the roles of adulthood as we play with authority, rules and leadership.

storylines can be evolving. Children are also communicating extensively about the play, discussing new rules and goals as the games evolve. Studies show that children can spend more time negotiating the rules of this style of play than actually playing the game. With one study recording around 80 per cent of the total playtime being devoted to a creative discussion of the rules (Figure 2.2).

However, with fewer opportunities to play together, children are not progressing through these stages of play as they once did. If your children seem unable to engage as you might expect them to, they may still need these earlier opportunities as they develop the skills required.

Understanding

Understand how important it is to retain children's opportunities for communication, movement and play – at any age!

When looking at ways of developing a child's learning we can become overly focused on the outcome we are looking to achieve. But when the brain processes information it does so in various ways. And we need to understand these processes if we are to effectively stimulate it. There is information we need to rapidly respond to that requires moment-to-moment, or rapid, attention. Such as when a cup falls off the table or being the first to answer a question before others get the right answer. And then there is information we need to concentrate on that requires sustained attention. Such as learning to read or writing a shopping list.

Every moment we need to rapidly move our focus, between rapid and sustained activities, scanning our visual and audible fields as we accurately and often subconsciously gather and process incoming sensory information. These are all skills that require the whole body working in unison and is something a developing child needs to learn and practice if they are to gain the skills to study for a test, to complete a task for a future boss or to plan and achieve any personal goal they set their mind to. However, if we are not careful, our children's time can become focused on one given activity, offering them little opportunity to use these skills to engage and consider the vast array of experiences they need. Whether this is through directed teaching approaches, heavily scheduled timetables of activity or a screen capturing their attention.

Communication

Children who have grown up within a communication rich environment will have heard in the range of 30 million more words by the time they start school than those children where communication was not valued or offered. Rehearsed through every exchange, the skills children need to develop depend on the amount of interactive conversation they are exposed to from an early age. But these need to be through human exchanges. While digital gaming may seem to involve connecting with friends, whether sat next to each other on the sofa or online, it does not directly engage one child with another like other forms of play. Or often, even involve them looking at another person. And a lack of these experiences is going to impact heavily on their communication skills now they are in the classroom.

Children who may be struggling to communicate may also be experiencing difficulties forming and maintaining friendships and may need help as they use language in their play. So, be sure to offer lots of one-to-one social exchanges that do not place them within the pressures of large group dynamics and be mindful of additional pressures their lack of communication may be placing on them. And then consider where children are getting these opportunities during the day. Do you value opportunities for discussion and peer collaboration? Are you mindful of making quieter areas available during free play? Do you frequently engage with children at their level, beyond the comments that are directed to the whole group? These are all golden opportunities for conversation, even if a child has yet to find words of their own.

Movement

Physical activity is a critically important aspect of every child's growth and development. From the moment a child is born, they are on an interconnected journey of development that will not be complete for many more years yet. Their minds and bodies are actively growing through every experience as muscles and bones strengthen and the connections in the brain are wiring up. When a child arrives at school their bodies are then still desperately trying to move as it uses all the physical actions necessary to grow and develop as it should.

This need for movement is embedded within all their methods of learning, not simply the fine and gross motor skills that may quickly come to mind. It is how they understand shape and space, how they train their eye muscles to focus on the words in a book and how they experience their thoughts and what they can do with them. This is why children can become so fidgety sitting on the floor during group activities, their body is telling them that they need to move. They need to explore their environment with bodies they can manage, they need to access the resources they require, with the fine motor skills to manage them. And they need to use their muscles and bones without becoming uncomfortable.

Now that a child finds themselves in a school classroom, none of these needs have changed. They are far from fully developed and no less in need of physical movement than they were a few years ago. The growth and the connections being made are essential for key messages to travel all around their body and without it, the next fundamental processes of development will be hampered. Excessive periods of time spent sitting in one position is preventing this work from happening, yet despite this children's opportunities for physical movement are likely to become more limited.

Play

An integral part of children's growth and development at every age, play nurtures a child's social and emotional maturity as well as every aspect of their cognitive and physical development. Play helps children adjust to the school setting, enhancing their readiness for the new expectations that will be placed on them. It also offers the peer interactions and joint enquiry that are all important components of establishing friendships and a growing sense of well-being. Research also repeatedly demonstrates unstructured play supporting all aspects of academic understanding and enhancing a child's ability to learn. Despite this, play can be significantly scheduled out of a child's day once other agendas come in.

The very nature of a child's learning sees it intertwined throughout interconnected processes of development. Let us consider the act of reading for example. As we rapidly take in the letters on the page, we are combining our visual skills with our knowledge of how to read as well as processing meaning from the things we are reading about. In addition to this, our brains need to guide our attention and our mental resources. Focusing continually and proactively on the task at hand as we stay focused for the required amount of time that we need. All the while being aware of our body as we sit upright, hold the book and know if we need to eat, drink or use the bathroom. Yet not jumping up every two minutes to get a snack. This is a lot to get right and it all needs practice.

When children play they are instantaneously utilising the interconnected skills of learning without needing to think about what they are doing or feeling like it's a chore. They are simultaneously mindful of their role in the play and the role of others, the rules that will be allowed and those that will break or stall the play and the resources and environments that are permitted. All the while being aware of their location and the permissions this implies. Do they need to listen out for a teacher's command to come in or the sound of a bell for the end of lunch? But this

Figure 2.3: During play, children rapidly utilise many interconnected skills in fun and enjoyable ways.

level of integration only comes from play that is both physical and social in nature, involving other children in ways that some may have limited experiences of (Figure 2.3).

Support

Be supported in developing teaching techniques that safeguard these opportunities for children, while engaging in rich and diverse learning experiences

When we think of an environment for learning, one particular image may spring to mind. It may be slightly different for each of us, but it probably does not change much from year to year or child to child. So, if this is the case, how do we stage an environment that is suitable for all the children that might come to learn within this space? Whilst every child is unique, their methods of learning and the core requirements that need to be established are not that dissimilar. Provided you remain aware of how children learn and the features that need to be in place for it to happen, you can then turn your attention to the individual child and how well they can access these features.

Communication

In Chapter 4 we will consider how to develop classrooms where children think and express themselves, so for now let us take a look at the environments and teaching strategies you can implement to support this process.

Children need to be able to listen and understand – However, not every child finds it easy to do either in a busy environment. If you have a child who is struggling, consider if they can focus given the level of background noise? Are they being expected to remember too many instructions? Do they understand the vocabulary you are using?

- Come down to a child's level and gain their attention before speaking to them

- Remind them that they need to use their "listening skills" and offer praise when you see the effort they use

- Speak clearly and slowly, using short, simple sentences with a pause between key phrases

- If possible, tell them what you are going to do before an activity, rather than during it. Especially if this involves anything practical or multi-staged

- You can also ask a child to repeat instructions back to you to ensure that they have heard and understood

- Be concise and to the point with what you want them to understand. For example "Please close your books," then allow them to do so before giving the next instruction

■ Think about the language you use as you try to be unambiguous and clear, repeating key words for emphasis

■ You can include visual supports such as picture cues or visual timelines

■ Children need time to process what they have heard and to be ready to do something with that information, so avoid rushing this process

■ If a child has not understood, repeat rather than rephrase which can add additional language to decipher

■ While open questions can be great to get children talking, for a child who is struggling this can be too much, so simplify

■ And be sure to reflect and summarise as you check for understanding.

Children need to see good communication modelled – Within a nurturing and interactive teaching environment that allows for frequent engagement and effective communication between adults and peers.

■ Allow children to interact, to work with and to become enthused by each other

■ Create a supportive environment where children feel comfortable to add their thoughts and ideas even when these are different to what is expected

■ Demonstrate an environment where anyone can ask a question, including you as you model that it is ok to ask for help

■ And remember to praise the effort they are putting into a task as you demonstrate that it is this, rather than any inherent "cleverness" that is resulting in their success

■ Encourage children to notice the efforts of their peers as they learn to recognise and appreciate the value of effort and how to spot it

■ Model active listening as you demonstrate to children how they can hear, respond and connect with others in the room.

Encourage children to find their voice – Not all children feel able to speak up within a group and may need some additional support and different teaching approaches.

■ Check in with less outspoken children to ensure they have all they need

■ Offer opportunities to work collaboratively within smaller groups

■ Through cooperative tasks, allow children to get a greater feel for what they are capable of

■ Come to them as you move around the space, rather than expecting children to communicate with the "teacher at the front" which can be somewhat intimidating

■ Avoid feeling like you always need to give a response, sometimes it is ok to simply listen

■ And above all, be sure to create a safe and supportive environment, where children feel able to speak in front of others, developing a greater confidence in what they have to say.

Movement

The more quality time children spend engaging in physical activity, playing together and enjoying time spent outdoors, the less chance there will be of them wanting to spend their every free moment in front of a screen. It certainly will not evaporate, but it will become less habit forming once alternatives are offered and sitting still stops becoming the default and automatic option. If you want to encourage this change for your children, talk to them. Explain the importance of getting active and the fun that it can be as you look to reduce the amount of time they spend sitting still as well as strategies to increase exercise.

Studies have shown that children who participate in regular physical activity tend to score better on a range of standardised academic achievement and IQ tests. With early indications that regular exercise results in increased formation of new synapses in the brain, especially when the activity is chosen for themselves. As well as the physical benefits of increased cardiovascular fitness, muscle tone, and improved skeletal strength, social physical activity has also been shown to have additional psychological and cognitive benefits (Figure 2.4).

However as you look to introduce more opportunities for movement, it is wise to remain mindful of the age of the children you are with. While a child is young they will be keen to try many things. You can then use this opportunity to introduce them to a wide range of activities as they get a feel for what they can do and what they might enjoy. For older children, you need not

Figure 2.4: With a few provocations, children need little encouragement to get physical.

assume they won't be interested, but be mindful of their age when you make suggestions to them. Avoid putting them in a situation where they will be judged against others or made to feel silly. As their social standing within the group becomes more important to them, they will avoid ways of feeling singled out. But there are many ways of getting active that do not involve public displays or competing directly against one another.

And while it is important to supply the resources for physical movement such as scooters and bikes, balls, rackets and hoops to develop the full range of basic movement skills, you also need to consider the time and space children are given to use them. If you feel confident that you have these two boxes ticked, consider how well staff are trained in understanding the need for physical activity and how to encourage it. And then be sure not to ruin all your hard work by keeping children in during physical activity time to sit and read. Or worse still, as a consequence for not behaving appropriately in class. It is often the children who need physical play the most who are kept in at lunch time.

Play

Today's children can find themselves with every free minute organised and diarised. Between school, after school activities, tennis lessons, swim team, piano practice and other enrichment activities, time to engage in free play can be effectively scheduled out. And once in school, this foundational method of learning can again be side-lined in favour of other demands, causing many children to disengage from learning at this time. A key aspect of my research and work with schools.

When time for play is permitted, it is technology that children from increasingly younger ages are reaching for. So, what do children gain from video gaming styles of play? Well, as you might expect, findings consistently show action video gamers to be faster at rapidly moving their attention than nonplayers. So much so that an Italian study successfully used video gaming to improve the visual abilities of dyslexic children, with enough of an effect to have a significant impact on their reading ability. However when it comes to sustained, proactively controlled attention, studies repeatedly suggest that screen time is negatively affecting children's ability to engage. As children's viewing times increase, the processes required to learn complex tasks are becoming significantly influenced. With researchers highlighting ongoing issues for children, causing problems that are affecting their long-term school performance and behaviour.

Children are hard-wired to play and every aspect of learning can be taught with an element of play. Helping them to develop an interest, to see relevance in the tasks you set and to ultimately learn much more quickly. So, combine these two things and you will automatically tap into these natural instincts and improve a child's level of engagement. If unused to playing freely, children may complain that they do not know what to do, or that they are bored when the opportunity is first given. Resist becoming involved at this point, autonomy and spontaneity are a critical part of the process. And provided you avoid comments that control or direct the play, which effectively takes their interest away, they will soon respond with bursts of creativity.

So, with every opportunity you have, look to offer every kind of play to your children as you support and encourage their development. Utilise the opportunities around you to bring playful learning into their day as you consider the physical elements that you can add to any lesson, allowing children to play with the ideas that you are introducing.

3 Helping children to feel safe and secure

Once children progress into the school classroom, consideration for the things they are learning may be centred around a given curriculum. You may have topics to follow or learning objectives that need to be accomplished. And yes, children will be learning continuously from the carefully designed experiences you are offering them, devised to accomplish these goals. But children are learning so much more than this.

Children are surrounded by learning opportunities; the ones you would like them to be having, as well as those you may not even be aware of. Whether you are managing a classroom full of children or home-schooling one child, they are hearing, seeing and picking up on the stimulus all around them. You may believe your children are taking no notice of the things you are saying to a friend or colleague, that they are not interested or are otherwise occupied. However, children are taking it all in... the good and the bad.

If a child hears exasperated comments about a child you are struggling with, they will be using this information when considering who to play with. If they see unintentional favouritism of certain groups when selecting who can go to lunch, they are picking up on cues that inform them about social order. And when particular children are repeatedly called on to respond to a question, they are establishing ideas about identity, their own voice and how much it is valued. From these lessons and the messages they are offering, children are then developing an increasingly established world view. Along with a strong idea of where they fit within it.

What's more, the spaces and environments you offer to your children may look and feel very different to them than you had intended. When they look around, do they feel like they belong here? Do they see themselves reflected in the words and images used? Is there evidence to show that they have spent time learning here and that this space belongs to them? Do they feel able to have an idea or an opinion? What if this is different to everyone else's? And can they access the areas and facilities they need at the time when they need them? Because stopping a child from using the bathroom will not stop them from needing it but it will stop them being able to think about anything else.

DOI: 10.4324/9781003327059-4

With these considerations in mind, we must then be aware of how a space feels to the individual children within it. When a child is given the respect they need, simply for being themselves, children learn to treat others with respect. When those that govern their environment are sensitive to their stage of development, children feel a greater sense of security within their care. And when the spontaneous responses and undeveloped physical needs that may need accommodating are recognised, these no longer hinder their progress. Instead, an emotional stability flourishes, allowing children to turn their attention to everything else that this safe and secure environment of learning is offering them (Figure 3.1).

Figure 3.1: From the moment children enter their classroom, they need to feel a part of it.

Knowledge

Know about the developing emotions and behaviours of children and how these are nurtured within the school classroom

As children's emotions and behaviours are maturing, more and more is being expected of them. But sometimes, rather than managing these greater expectations in their stride, children can seem to take a step backwards. Struggling with the demands placed on them they can revert to the behaviours and tendencies of a time when they felt more comfortable. And in a busy classroom where the pace and ratios may be ill-equipped for managing this, the exasperation and frustration a child feels around them can add to their feelings of anxiety.

However, children who are surrounded by adults who are sensitive to their needs are going to feel more comfortable in their care. If they are given the time and understanding to acclimatise to the people, environments and demands they now find themselves surrounded by, they are more likely to settle. And when they feel a part of this experience, rather than it being something that is happening to them, they are more likely to grow, not decline within it.

Developing a sense of who they are

When children transition into the school classroom they are beginning a very different stage of their learning journey. As familiar as the school classroom may seem to you, for a child it represents something monumental. Within this new environment they will be developing a new sense of who they are as they take on the identity of the "school child." This new image of themselves is so important that it may come with a new appearance (school uniform), important belongings (lunch box, school bag) and expectations (homework, reading practice). It certainly involves a new location, possibly a different journey and a whole group of new people, environments and expectations.

As a child begins to experience what this new persona feels like, they will be making subconscious decisions as to how this new identity fits them. Are they suited to being a "school child"? Are they any good at it? Is this somewhere that feels right that they can thrive within and feel good about? Is it somewhere that they can add something to with the skills and abilities they can offer? When children begin to show reluctance about going to school, when they proclaim, "I don't like it!" "It's boring" or "I don't feel well, I think I need to stay at home," it is often a good indication that something within this process is failing them.

Throughout this series of books, I have made the point that children are born learning and continue to do so every minute of every day. They are actively inquisitive and keen to understand from the moment they draw breath. And with so much to learn they are born with intrinsic methods hardwired to support this process. However, these methods are not always in keeping with their experiences of learning in the school classroom.

■ Children are physical learners; they need to move with their whole bodies

■ Children are social learners; they need to talk to and work with others, sharing what they and others are doing and validating their own efforts

■ Children are experiential learners; they need to experience what they are learning, not simply be told about it

■ Children learn in the moment; they have rapidly evolving ideas that are not yet fully formed yet need exploring and expressing.

To the child that is asked to sit nicely, to not talk to the child next to them and to listen to the lesson presented from the board, this goes against every hardwired inclination. And the lesson being taught becomes "You are not suited to this environment; you don't fit the persona of the good school child".

Developing social behaviours

We all need to feel a part of a group, that we are connected to a reliable set of supportive people that we can depend upon. For a child who has just begun in their new class, either at the beginning of the school year or following a move, this sense of belonging is paramount. I grew up with a father in the forces and moves every couple of years were a way of life. So, feeling like an outsider is a very strong childhood memory for me, as is the insecurity that comes along with it.

Before developing a sense of belonging within the environment, thoughts cannot turn to the content of the lesson or the expectations placed on a child. So, working towards any higher order thinking will probably be a fool's errand. Instead, turn your attentions to their sense of belonging with some joint activities or group exercises, working in pairs or sharing key times. The trust and sense of security that will be growing in these moments is fundamental to a child's well-being, showing them that they have a supportive network around them. It helps them to forge new relationships and make friends within the group. And as these connections are made, it establishes a sense of belonging; to people, to environments and to practices that they can feel confident in.

When children enter the school classroom for the first time, many will be coming from the environments of free movement and play that are common to the early years. No longer permitted to move about or engage freely with other children whenever they choose, being assigned a desk space or a spot on the carpet may come as quite a shock. And at a time of great change, this can leave them feeling vulnerable and alone. Especially when they are hardwired, as we all are, to be social learners, reaching out to others and learning with them as they learn to support others in return.

Children also need opportunities to engage in their learning, recognising what they can do and celebrating in the abilities they can demonstrate to others. Through these processes, children are experiencing the relevance of the efforts they are putting into something, long before they have reached mastery. They are learning to trust in their abilities as a learner and what they can achieve. They are also learning how everyone experiences setbacks and how these are simply another opportunity for learning.

Feeling safe and secure means having a sense of control; of yourself and the environment

By the very nature of being a child, children will often experience a lack of control throughout their day. While much of this is a necessary part of keeping them safe and well cared for, in other respects it may be a result of habit or expectation. But imagine for a moment how safe and secure you would feel if someone took away your control. Now imagine if this were in an environment that you were not familiar with and with people and expectations you neither knew nor understood.

While you will need to make many decisions for children, they also need to explore what they are capable of. They need to challenge their boundaries, developing the courage to push their limits. They need to discover what they are capable of and who they are as a learner. And they cannot do this if they are constantly managed. Without any influence on the direction or outcome of their efforts, how can they develop confidence in their abilities? How can they learn to handle their problems, to overcome setbacks or to keep going even during the times when it doesn't come easy? (Figure 3.2)

Giving children a sense of control means giving them a level of autonomy over what they are doing, the approaches they are taking and when. It means allowing them to access the environment and its resources as and when they need to and to engage with other children. Within these moments children are developing a sense of who they are and what they are capable of. They are developing a sense

Figure 3.2: Children need to feel a sense of autonomy within their learning and environment as they make choices and explore what they can do.

of self-reliance and independence that they will later rely on. And they are learning what it means to have a sense of their own power, to try as hard as they can, to push themselves through challenges and to manage difficult situations.

Understanding

Understand how children's emotions can feel, how difficult they can be to express and the fallout that might be experienced

Children can arrive for their first day of school with many different experiences behind them. We have all seen the impact of global pandemics, universal shutdowns and limited socialisation. What we haven't yet seen is the long-term effects that COVID-19 will have on this generation of children who experienced their early childhood with increased levels of stress in the home, lifestyle restrictions, increased dependence on screen-time and the widespread use of masks impacting early speech and language development. With limited socialisation, home-schooling and home caring, along with parents and siblings working in the home, early childhood was unrecognisable for many. But it doesn't stop there.

Reduced opportunities for physical activity saw limitations in children's core muscle development, flexibility and balance. While limited social interactions introduced additional challenges with sharing and turn taking, poor communication skills and a limited vocabulary. With every experience we have feeding into our next, there is real concern for children's emotional resilience, their speaking and listening skills and general levels of self-confidence. Now, more than ever, we must be considering children's prior experiences while we are considering our expectations of them as we look to understand the mechanisms driving children's emotions, behaviours and responses.

Helping children to feel their emotions

Emotions are a part of everyone's lives and if they are avoided or seen as an obstacle or difficulty to be controlled, this does little to teach children how to manage them. And if they remain unmanaged, avoided or worse masked with medications, more difficult behaviours will simply become entrenched. Now as children reach an age where they can begin recognising their emotions, they can begin to acknowledge them and understand how they are making them feel. While this might seem like a daunting prospect, especially in the middle of a school classroom, this is an essential part of the process if children are going to learn how to manage their growing emotions for themselves.

For children who have experienced an early childhood full of heightened emotion and stress, their brain development will have adapted to manage within these surroundings. Having previously detected heightened fear and worry, they have adapted to be ready to react at a moment's notice. However, sitting within a classroom where they are required to concentrate and pay attention with more stable emotions, they may struggle. These children are often found to react with heightened emotions, quick to cry, to appear helpless or to react with anger. This level of focus and excess energy is also exhausting. It can limit a child's ability to concentrate and maintain attention and may affect their behaviours in ways that are similar, and often confused with the signs of Conduct Disorder (CD) and Attention Deficit Hyperactivity Disorder (ADHD).

With excessive levels of stress now linked to the stem cause of many diseases and with the long-term psychological and emotional effects of unmanaged stress on children frequently documented, your instinct may be to wade in and manage these situations yourself. But a more helpful response in the long-term is to recognise what is happening, to help children understand their emotions and to offer them methods of recognising and managing their behaviours for themselves. Before the need for potentially lifelong and little understood medications which are increasingly becoming a reality for many children.

Defining children's behaviours through everything you say and do

When you spend real quality time with children, engaging in two-way, quality conversations from day one, you are building trusted connections and attachments. These are being used to build a sense of the relationship they have with you and what they can expect from you. They are also informing the child of how they think you see them. These messages are so powerful, they stay with children through all the moments when you are not around, imprinting on them as their most enduring role model within this space. Through all your conscious and mostly unconscious behaviours, habits and reactions. So, be mindful of how and where you attach your strongest drivers, as it is this that will tend to surface, influencing your focus on the day and as a result, how your children will respond (Figure 3.3).

As they establish a sense of who they are within the classroom, children will tend to "'do as you do", far more often than they will "do as you say". By

Figure 3.3: Through every engagement you are building powerful attachments with a child.

being empathetic and emotionally available to your children you can model the behaviours you would like to see. Show them how you express your thoughts and ideas. Do not be afraid to let them see you grapple with the learning process as you seek answers, a better understanding or a new skill. Let them see your enjoyment in applied learning as you take topics and concepts into real situations. And talk with your children about different situations as you help them to see the world through another person's eyes.

But this does not come from conversations or lesson plans predesigned, delivered and driven solely by you. With the understanding boiled down into "who can answer this question" style discussions. In this scenario, children are missing out on the wide range of possibilities that learning in its wider sense can offer and can feel like they either "measure up", or not. And with every assessment they experience, this dual notion of their identity is further underlined. The messages children are receiving and the ways they are learning to see themselves are imprinting throughout early and middle childhood. Reinforced through the behaviours they see role modelled by the trusted adults they continuously look to, showing them how they should behave in the world. As well as seeking the beliefs and values they should live by, all of which stay with them, informing the choices they later make.

Confusion over thinking for themselves or doing as they are told

Accepting and taking ownership of behaviour is a difficult lesson to learn and one that you need to support your children in. But only when a child is allowed to think for themselves can they be held responsible for their actions. And when you are trying to teach them how you would like them to behave, this is an important part of the process. To be capable of thinking for themselves, children need to know that they have a voice, that it is respected and listened to. But this becomes impossible if a child is confused over the power they have to decide on their actions. You do then need to show them that you trust them to think for themselves, that they have choice over their behaviours and ownership of the consequences. And that you are there for support and guidance should they need it.

Children who are surrounded with conversations and debate have been shown to be significantly better at engaging in empathy-based reasoning for themselves. And where questions about what could happen next are being openly discussed with explanation, children are far more likely to engage in prosocial behaviours when an adult is not around to monitor. This is infinitely more powerful than telling a child to behave or offering threats if they do not.

If you do not want children to raise their voices or to appear like they are not listening to you, maybe consider how your behaviours are being interpreted by them. How you respond to your children during a moment of conflict has a massive impact, affecting not only their external behaviours but also the ways in which they think, feel, and even manage their future emotions. So, support your children as they learn everything they need to know about the choices they are making and the consequences that come with them as they experience the power this offers.

Support

Be supported to offer children the understanding and guidance they need, rooted in an informed understanding of their feelings of security

In our modern, technology rich and fast paced world, increasing numbers of children are struggling, experiencing depression, bullying, behavioural problems, drug and alcohol related abuse and suicide. Now, more than ever we need to actively consider the environments and opportunities we surround our children with and the sense of safety and security this is offering to them.

With studies linking the amount of time children have for free play to their happiness, their level of self-esteem and their development of self-awareness, we need to actively find ways of offering this mainstay of childhood to our children. But if a struggling child experiences more time spent in academic catch up than playing with friends, we need to ask ourselves what impact this is having, both now and in the long-term? If children are stopped from experiencing a childhood or are no longer given the time or social connections to engage, these are worrying times for all the rich processes of development that our children need.

Giving them time to find who they are

Supporting our children to develop in the best ways possible has been the aspiration of parents, carers and teachers for centuries. Although it is good to encourage and enrich a child's development in reading, maths or creativity, there is something lost if we push beyond "supporting" to "hurrying". Children need their childhood to progress at their own pace, mastering things when they are ready with the time they need.

Feeling emotionally safe depends on the type of attachment style you have been given the opportunities to develop. But it also depends on the relationship dynamics that have been created with the people around you. And this involves feeling at ease expressing your ideas and what you really think. It means feeling comfortable when being in a place of vulnerability and feeling emotionally secure without constant reassurance. So, as much as you might be tempted to run and hide during a Tuesday morning meltdown, the coping strategies you share early on are equipping your children with emotion regulation skills. Long before their vulnerable teenage years when a voice of reason may not be so easily on hand.

But this needs for you to notice your children's emotions for what they are. Listening and responding to their anxieties and concerns in caring and constructive ways as you help them practice self-recognition, empathy and active management. Helping children to avoid riskier ways of dealing with their emotions when you are not around. But first they need to be able to feel them in a safe and secure environment. Children who experience environments where emotions are expressed in healthy ways are more likely to use healthy coping strategies when their own emotions feel triggered, affecting the way that they manage stress and anxiety.

Feeling safe and secure

To support children in managing their emotions, you need to first consider how you manage and model your own. Do you recognise and name your feelings? Do you address conflicts by demonstrating responsible and purposeful techniques? Or do you simply manage the situation in front of you, allowing unresolved issues to resurface, spilling out over those who least deserve it? When a situation is becoming fraught with emotions, it is important that we take a breath and show children how they can actively take steps to go back to a state of calm, demonstrating how they can deal with emotional situations or conflicts. With every comment and interaction, your children are learning about their world and how the people in it behave. If you are experiencing some difficult behaviours, consider where these influences may be coming from. Help your children to learn how to mentally take another person's perspective on a situation by noticing situations in which someone needs some help, in their play, in a book or in something you watch together.

As a young child, a teenager and all the years to come, feeling safe and secure fundamentally means the same thing. It is about having your emotional needs met. It is about feeling confident about who you are, without feeling the need to unfavourably compare yourself to others. It is about having the ability to take care of yourself or feeling secure in the knowledge that others will take care of you. And it is about having an element of control in your life. Without these fundamental things in place, a person is going to struggle. And once in that state, thoughts and attention will be on little else (Figure 3.4).

As children get older, they are more likely to seek these things from their peers than they are from their parents, teachers or other adults around them. Along with any advice and direction they feel they need. But for the time being, the words and actions you are putting in place are having a significant impact on a child's

Figure 3.4: We all need to feel safe and secure within our environments before we can function on any higher level. For some children, that may require a little more patience and understanding.

sense of safety and security. And will continue to resonate with them long after you are no longer the biggest influence on their lives. And it is these underpinning messages that will continue to inform and reinforce children's emotional responses and the likelihood of their future behaviours. For this reason it is essential that we are mindful of our influence when we engage with children. Paying close attention to the time we give them and the value they feel we offer them.

■ **Find time for each child** – In a busy classroom it can be easy for a child to slip through the net and go all day without real, quality time. Think about every child and the opportunities they had this week to talk to you, to laugh, share some news or a thought on a one-to-one level. While this might be about the learning, it certainly does not have to be. And remember, not every child feels like sharing within the larger group

■ **Show them some warmth and affection** – This can be anything from a kind word to a warm smile. Children need to feel valued and important to you and what may seem like a small gesture can make all the difference in the world

■ **Listen** – Children have a lot to say. Just not necessarily in the ways you might expect. When you hear what a child is saying you can learn to uncover the deep thinking and lateral leaps in their understanding that it might contain. Provided you don't dismiss all but the answer you were expecting

■ **Offer meaningful praise** – Discussed in more detail in a previous book in this series, praise of the right things at the right time offers children a pivotal boost to their self-esteem and self-worth. By praising that which they have some control over, like the effort they are putting into a task, you support the confidence they require to flourish

■ **Model the behaviours you want to see** – All of them. And this includes laughter and fun, as well as respect and understanding. Children are learning from all of your behaviours, even the ones you might rather they had not picked up on

■ **Be clear where the boundaries are** – Children need freedoms and autonomy, but they also need clear and consistent boundaries in order to feel secure. Establish these early on, preferably with the children's input and ensure they remain fair and reliably enforced

■ **Recognise them and all they are** – Every child is unique and special in their own way. They are so much more than a set of learning objectives to be met at the end of the year, so celebrate all their talents and skills, their thoughts and ideas.

4 Developing classrooms where children think and express themselves

Through a combination of decision-making opportunities, responsibility and experiences of having their thoughts genuinely heard, children can experience what it means to think for themselves and to know what the power of their thoughts and actions mean. They can also learn to hear and understand the thoughts of others, even when these are different to their own. When you give children a voice they are able to explore their ideas, they are more likely to stand up for themselves, to act in their own best interest and exercise their rights. And as they get older they are less likely to be easily led, seeking the approval of their peers.

Within the safety of childhood, you give children these opportunities when you trust them to make age appropriate and meaningful decisions. With your guidance they can learn to respect the rights and legitimate needs of themselves and others. And if some children are strong-willed, celebrate in this strength of will, knowing that the independent thinking you are fostering will serve them well through their later years as they will be far less easily swayed by the influences around them when you are not there to guide.

When you allow your children to experience making their own decisions, either alone or with a small group of peers, you empower them through the sense of responsibility that you offer. And as they see the results of their decisions, you are offering them lasting memories of what they can achieve. Within this process they are learning even through their mistakes, as poor choices become a step on their learning journey. In an environment where they can constructively work through their ideas, you can teach children to be responsible and resourceful. And when they encounter problems or differing opinions, they can learn to become a resilient and powerful individual with self-esteem, integrity and a sense of their own purpose.

Within a classroom dynamic, many decisions and responsibilities will remain with the adults. But as you read this chapter, take a moment and consider your justifications

DOI: 10.4324/9781003327059-5

for the rules and processes you have in place. Consider where children can experience making some of these decisions for themselves. Where can they learn what taking responsibility feels like? How do they learn to know and manage consequences? And where rules and decisions do remain with you, how do you use these to demonstrate your thinking and the reasoning behind them?

Knowledge

Know the importance of allowing children the time and space to think for themselves and the impact this has on their learning potential

From the moment a child is born they are looking at the world and trying to make sense of it. Now they find themselves in a fascinating, new learning environment, with a bewildering array of things to take in, to learn and make sense of. Luckily all their deeply rooted instincts to learn and understand remain with them, as their brains, eager to understand are learning through every experience. It is then of great importance that children experience a wide range of activities and learning opportunities throughout their years of formal education. Together with the time, space, opportunities and permissions they need to make sense of them.

What are we teaching children for?

When you stop and ask yourself "What is the point of education, what are we actually doing here?" I am sure, like me, many responses will come to mind. There will be knowledge and understanding of many things on that list, along with ways of preparing children for futures we cannot yet understand. As they go out into the world, they will be responding to the people and places they find themselves surrounded by. They will be combining new information in different ways and making decisions when trusted adults are no longer around to safeguard them. They do then need to know things, yes, but they also need to know how to think for themselves, to apply new information in ways that are right and meaningful for them. And before they are given more complex ways of using their own free will, they need to have learnt ways of exercising this in appropriate ways.

When we allow our children opportunities to make their own decisions, they can experience what it means to think for themselves, making their own choices before these become subject to peer pressure or a risk of harm. They learn to use the wealth of information around them, combining this with the knowledge, skills and previous experiences you have offered them as they make their own choices. Whilst the root they take may be surprising or the outcome unexpected, these processes are allowing children to develop a far deeper understanding of what they are capable of. Along with a developing understanding of the potential consequences (Figure 4.1).

Given a degree of autonomy within their tasks and the rate they progress through them, children also find it easier to focus their attention and engage. This is further enhanced when they are given an element of choice over who they engage with and the spaces they occupy. Offering children a voice and with it, a sense

Figure 4.1: Part of learning is about making connections with what we know, adding our own ideas and those of others and seeing what we are capable of.

of responsibility, is then something that we need to embrace throughout a child's education. Through learning experiences carefully selected for their current stage of development and with resources they are free to explore and governed by their interest and curiosity. As their development progresses, new materials, ideas and techniques can then be introduced, all within orderly spaces where children experience a sense of responsibility and ownership.

The time and permission to think

Children need time to absorb new knowledge. The brain needs to process it, challenge it against what it thought it knew, make links and rearrange previous understanding. It needs to trial this new knowledge in different contexts, with different variables as it makes connections and thinks about what has been learnt. When you give children opportunities to express their thoughts and opinions, you can see this in action as they apply their developing skills through creative responses, making their own decisions and acting on their new knowledge.

As children develop in mind and body, they are also establishing a sense of who they are and formulating an idea of how they fit within the environment they find themselves in. If, through our teaching styles, we seem to only value one response or dismiss their thoughts into what might be a deeper insight into their understanding simply because it deviated from our expectations, their developing capabilities and sense of self can be easily hurt, wounded, distorted or even devastated. Children need opportunities to voice their thoughts, even when these include misconceptions or illustrate problems. But to do this, they need to feel comfortable making errors and expressing what they think.

In an environment where mistakes are considered a valuable part of the learning journey, children can experience failing without losing confidence. They can learn to use this experience as they understand where the gaps in their knowledge are, learning different approaches, reconsidering what they think they know and adapting it as new information suggests inconsistencies or potential errors. But to do this, children need time to reflect on what they are learning, with opportunities to use what they have learnt before transitioning on to the next task.

If this time is taken away, children only experience the "less than perfect" stage of the learning process, before receiving more instruction, further information or being forced to give up on a task before they reach a point of feeling comfortable. This will then encourage a similar response the next time they are met with a less than perfect experience of their knowledge or skills.

How our approaches are impacting this learning potential

When you teach using the same techniques and methods for every child, every day this allows strong pathways and networks to be established deep inside the brain. While this might sound like a good idea for some things, after all, children all need to know the same letters, the same numbers and what they need to do with them. However, if we extend this to all learning, do we really want another generation knowing and thinking in exactly the same ways when the world is a dramatically different place to be? What does this say for our children's future or indeed that of our society? How will this result in children reaching their full potential when they have not seen the possibilities of it? How will they experience original thought or creativity? Where will they find any deeper meaning if they have no experience of searching for it?

Whilst there are of course lessons that need to be taught, boundaries that need to be in place and certain rules that will sometimes be imposed, children do not need to be told what to think. Do you really have the same values and beliefs as the adults that were around you when you were growing up? Or do your views differ from your parents now that you live in a vastly different world than they did? As strong, influential adults in our children's lives, we must be careful of the views and opinions we impose on our children. Whether this is through actions and responses we are not aware of or by simply correcting a child when they are trying to express a different response.

If you want a child to know how to think, to be naturally curious about themselves and the world around them and to not be easily swayed by a peer group, they need opportunities to question and to drive their own responses rather than expecting to be led. And if you want a child to grow up with integrity and autonomy, they need opportunities to make their own choices and their own mistakes. They need to learn about what is expected of them and to see that their choices have consequences. Whilst at the same time seeing their mistakes as useful learning opportunities, rather than something to be feared or hidden away. And to do this, they need to be a part of the learning process, with thoughts and ideas that are listened to and acknowledged rather than experiencing the learning process as something that happens to them.

Understanding

Understand the environments and styles of interaction children need to develop their abilities to think and the confidence to express these thoughts

As was explored in previous books in this series, young children are in the process of finding out what it means to have a voice, developing the confidence to think for themselves and learning what it means to express an opinion. But this is a complex process that they are only just beginning to explore. Sometimes their thoughts will not be fully formed before they are voiced. They wouldn't have thought through all options and they certainly would not have considered every outcome. This process is more like the "thinking out loud" we might engage in. The trouble comes however when children's developing thoughts are missed for not offering the expected answer that a closed question or busy environment might invite. Regardless of the great ideas, the emerging connections or the leaps of understanding in their learning that their comments might suggest.

If you have ever felt being dismissed in this way, imagine how this feels to a child who is in the process of finding their voice and developing their confidence to use it. Now think how secure you might feel tomorrow when considering voicing another opinion, idea or your growing understanding in front of the group.

Throughout all stages of development, it is essential that we retain realistic expectations of our children, of their developing maturity, their capabilities and their intentions. Growing up is all about experiencing our choices and the consequences of them as we learn and grow through them. If we want our children to be responsible, resourceful, resilient human beings they need to have trust in themselves and this comes from us firstly showing trust in them. Unnecessary questions, constant governance of their actions and direction of their experiences damages this trust when children need support, explanation, encouragement and opportunities to experience, to think and to grow (Figure 4.2).

Figure 4.2: From the very first time a child ventures an opinion in their school classroom, they need to feel that their ideas are valid, even if a little unexpected.

Understanding what children need

As parents and educators it is important that we put our minds back and remember what it was like to be a child, experiencing new environments for the very first time. Seeing the reactions of people you do not yet know with limited experience of reading them. Hearing instructions or questions that you do not fully understand and feeling lost as to what to do next. While you may have many more recent memories of this, perhaps a recent move or job change, there is a huge difference between your experience of this and that of the children around you who do not have the voice or choice to do much about it. Children are also driven by very different desires. They are informed by a unique agenda and with an as yet unformed understanding of time, empathy or consequence. Simply by virtue of their age and their experiences, these processes are not as well informed by past experiences. And they have a very different way of processing their thoughts than you do.

To understand what they should do next, children are absorbing all the additional cues they need from you and the world around them. They are also making complex links in their learning between what has gone on before, assimilating the new and deciding whether to incorporate or reject. This may require lots of revisiting, going back to things that have been put away or were not on the plan for today's session. But if you keep all of this in mind, you can be careful not to miss out on the vast array of thought and conscious inquiry that is taking place outside of your learning objectives.

Practice that understands what it means to be a child

When you consider the children whose lives you are moulding every day, you can be forgiven for thinking firstly of the set of learning goals assigned for the calendar age they have now reached. When confronted daily with the objectives placed on us, it is all too easy to forget that our job is so much more complex than imparting a set of abilities into a child, preparing them for the next transition, ready to prove themselves capable.

Children are thinking, feeling individuals, processing all the influences around them from the first day we meet them. However, they are not little adults. Even into their teenage years, they are moving through fluid and malleable processes as they grow into the person they will become. Comments and actions of well-meaning adults can easily be misinterpreted, creating distortions which, if continuous, can impact their well-being in the moment. And if prolonged, have devastating effects on their developing personality. How many adults do you know with a story about a comment that was made to them as a child and the huge impact it had?

Children do require guidance, together with age-appropriate freedoms, all within a context of trust. They need to experience security, without being overcontrolled and surrounded by adults who are both gracious and understanding. Their depth of thinking capability and individual potential needs believing in and stimulating every day within an environment that allows for self-discovery and the space to engage in the challenges of learning in a resilient way. But they also need our careful explanations and encouragement and for us to offer them opportunities to experience, to think and to develop a robust and resilient sense of themselves as capable learners.

Nurturing children's thoughts

If we want our children to be responsible, resourceful, resilient human beings they need to have trust in themselves and this comes from us firstly showing trust in them. Circumventing or sidestepping their questions, overruling their ideas with our pre planned objectives or assuming the "I'm the adult, I know best" approach damages this trust and discourages any tendency toward independent thought. Instead, children need our belief in them, our support and to feel safe within a structured environment, where they can offer their opinion without feeling dismissed, over controlled or often dismissed.

When children experience a combination of decision-making opportunities and responsibilities within the safety of childhood, they can lay the foundations for the executive functions to follow. Becoming more aware of what they think and feel they are far less easily swayed by the influences around them when you are not there to guide. They are more likely to act in their own best interest, to stand up for themselves and exercise their rights and respect the rights and legitimate needs of others. Whereas children who have experienced limited opportunities or who have frequently had adults' step-in do not feel secure within their own abilities. Feeling unsafe within unfamiliar situations, this can often cause them to shy away from new experiences and give up on a challenge. Lacking self-esteem and a sense of their own power, this can be a risky place to be (Figure 4.3).

Figure 4.3: Given opportunities to work in small groups, to trial their ideas and see what works, children gain a greater understanding of what it means to have a voice.

Nurturing children's confidence to express themselves

Children at every age need a safe environment in which to grow; emotionally, socially and academically as they gain a sense of who they are. They need to be accepted and respected when this growth and development brings with it differences from what you may have been expecting. They may be interested in something completely different to what you had planned this week. They may take longer to master something others are finding easy. But they will respond best when they can express themselves openly. When they can explore their own choices and when all of this can happen without feeling themselves being hurried. Children also need the opportunity to learn from their own decisions, rather than having things done for them. They will look to you for guidance and support, but an overbearing "helicopter" style of teaching will diminish a child's capacity to cope with challenges when you are not there to assume that control.

As they go out into the world, making decisions and voicing their opinions without a trusted adult "safety net", they will be doing so with their own free will. An ability to know their own mind, to think for themselves and to choose to do the right thing during their teenage years will see them less likely to be swayed by undesirable influences. Or easily led by seeking the approval of their peers. Exercising their freewill in appropriate ways is then a complex technique that needs to be learnt and practised throughout childhood. But whilst this is a tricky thing to accomplish, celebrate in a child's strength of will while they have strong ideas and opinions about everything. Knowing that the independent thinking you are fostering will serve them well through their later years. And let's face it, we all have our [pink, permed, shaved] hair story from our teenage years that we would rather forget.

Support

Be supported in developing the practices and environments children need to think and express themselves

So how do we go about doing this? How do we encourage children to think for themselves within an environment of learning objectives and lesson plans? How do we understand what they find interesting? How can we give them opportunities to explain, discuss and deliberate? And all as they are learning from the tone of your voice, your gestures and displayed emotions, as much as anything you may have planned within the content of the lesson. Children will be watching your considered actions as well as the unconscious decisions you make. All of which is telling them so much about how this social world of learning works and how much they feel a part of it.

Learning from the decisions being made

Firstly, look to engage children in the thinking process and encourage their reflections. The "Do it the way I am telling you" approach does little more than foster boredom. How interested are you in the tasks you have to do every day? How about the tasks you want to do or are particularly interested in? Offering children an investigation where they can apply the knowledge you have given them in different ways allows them to explore these ideas for themselves. And when they do not turn out quite as expected, the learning process is enhanced in a number of ways.

■ Firstly through the cognitive application of knowledge – joining hands and minds is a hugely powerful way of learning

■ Secondly as they work on the task, they are becoming more invested in its outcome and therefore more interested in the effects they are having on it

■ And thirdly, you are giving them a memory of the experience.

Think back to your experiences of learning, how many "No, you are not right" messages do you remember and how rich are the memories of applying the experience? You can be "told" that overfilling the coffee machine will end in a mess to clear up, the memory of having done it will be far stronger.

Learning by thinking more deeply

Next, help children to think more deeply by considering questions and problems which require deeper reasoning and explanation. Questions that invite conversation can also be used, where alternative responses can be considered; "What do you think might

happen if...?" "What do you think would be a good way to..." These can then be followed by investigations where children explore their thoughts and ideas, along with a period of reflection; "Were your results surprising?" "Did you change your mind?" And as you consider the questions you pose to them, ensure they require more than a quick answer. Then give the time to really get involved as they ponder their responses. Many children find it difficult to talk out loud in a large group, volunteering suggestions that they might yet be unsure of. Offering opportunities to talk first with a partner or to discuss in small groups can give them more confidence in coming forward.

Learning by managing mistakes

Then consider how you and your children view their mistakes or perceived wrong turns. Is there any negative talk of

Figure 4.4: Utilising a range of resources to explore how the Three Little Pigs should build a strong house, there can be no "wrong" answer, only lessons learnt.

failure, disappointment or self-criticism? Or do you take this opportunity to celebrate in the learning that has happened, thinking about the experience that can be learnt from for next time and the potential for further growth and understanding? Whilst the former is helping them to construct a negative spiral, reinforcing a sense of failure or inadequacy that will be carried forward into any future attempts, the latter will allow them to take this setback as a call-to-arms, helping them to see where they can learn more within what is an ongoing journey (Figure 4.4).

Learning by finding their voice

Children learn to express themselves by having the opportunity to do it; in safe environments where they are confident that their opinion will be heard and listened to. Even if it differs from everyone else's. And the best way to enrich an expressive environment for your children to become involved in is to ensure that certain voices are not dominating. Every child, even the quiet ones, need to develop their voice, and the more vocal children need to learn how to restrain it. Children need to trial their voice within pair discussions and small groups as they get instant feedback on how they are doing, before being expected to contribute in front of a whole class. So, offer children rich language opportunities and enjoy the fun and the benefits that communication and sharing in everyone's thinking can bring.

Learning by recognising the thoughts of others

By five-years of age children are getting better at understanding the thoughts and emotions of others. They can imagine the emotions of fictional characters that you may read about in a shared story or the puppets or characters you use to tell one. By eight-years old they can understand that people can feel differently about the same situation. And by nine to twelve years, they can imagine how someone else might think about a situation they themselves have never encountered. But all of this takes practice and experience of hearing what others might think about a situation. So, utilise this within the experiences you are offering and encourage children as they share their thoughts and feelings together.

And a final word

Children are frequently directed, in their actions, their location and their experiences. But as you go through the day, try to connect with them on their level, as you get to know them from where they are. This can be tough with a room full of children who are all changing at a rapid rate. So, listen to what they have to say with empathy and concern.

■ Take delight in your children as they crave your attention and approval. And give it as freely as you can

■ Be gentle in your corrections as you redirect them back toward desired behaviours

■ Support them to master new skills and be enthusiastic about their progress

■ Help them to resist automatically looking to others for approval, as they learn to value their own judgement instead

■ Help them trust when they feel good about something, regardless of popular opinion

■ Find something they genuinely care about and help them to see their strengths as well as areas of improvement

■ Then help them to realistically set goals and recognise their achievements.

Children will experience difficult times growing up – it is a part of the journey. But you have a unique opportunity while they are with you, to offer them a protective influence. Every time you remain open to seeing and hearing them, you are showing them they matter. Even if you cannot understand the magnitude of feelings they might be expressing. Constant comparisons or expectations beyond their years is affecting all our children, when all they really want is to be loved and valued exactly as they are, not how they could be. So, embrace their unique ways of thinking and the insight this gives you into their developing mind. Be careful of the language you use as you encourage their confidence rather than denting their self-esteem. And foster a belief in the power of their thoughts and opinions that they can carry forward into future experiences.

5 Understanding child anxiety

Teaching young children can sometimes feel like a minefield of important things you need to get just right. You may have all the experience and books written on how to do it all; you may have even read most of them. Unfortunately, a seemingly over-wrought and anxious child frustrated at their lack of skill in today's task of choice has not. In these moments, as we want to make them feel like everything is good with their world once again, we may find ourselves saying and doing things without the considered, reflective approaches that we might wish to use. But where do you begin? Children need, more than anything, to grow up in a place of safety and security. However, while we think we are offering them just that, they will be picking up on so much more than our chosen words, and this includes our own anxieties.

We know ourselves that feelings of anxiety can escalate when we do not know what is happening to us. When we do not feel in control of the situation we are in or if we are not fully aware of all the facts. Now imagine this for a child who will often feel this lack of control in their lives. When they do not understand what is happening or what will happen next, their anxiety can become even more pronounced. However stressful a situation may be, feelings of guilt, confusion or a lack of control will only add to this. And on top of this, they may not have the voice or opportunity to do much about it alone.

The truth is, no matter how old you are or the circumstances of your life, stress and anxiety is experienced by us all from time to time. And while the cause of the stress and the ways in which it shows itself may look quite different, left unchecked it can be devastating. Affecting eating, sleeping and healthy development on all levels and in ways that are causing serious long-term effects. Add to that a lack of time to be calm and still, to simply allow the matters of the day to settle and it is no wonder our growing children are experiencing increased emotional, social and cognitive stresses. However, stressful events are and will always be a very real part of everyone's life and it is in understanding this anxiety and its roots that this chapter will look to explore.

DOI: 10.4324/9781003327059-6

Knowledge

Know where child anxiety can come from, how to recognise it and steps you can take to help children with it

In today's chaotic, fast-paced and uncertain world, our children are having a tough time. Many are experiencing difficulties from an ever earlier age, with increasing numbers of children displaying hypersensitive behaviours, anxiety and stress related illness, triggered by the increased emotional, social and cognitive stresses they are under. The result of all this is children as young as three being prescribed sleeping medication and children under five receiving antidepressants. Other studies are connecting this sense of disconnection to a rise in childhood obesity, depression, emotional instability and mental illnesses. It is affecting our children's abilities to regulate their emotions and their energy levels. It is also having a huge impact in the classroom where research consistently shows us, children need to feel safe and secure to do well.

With more children receiving diagnosis for ADHD, diabetes, obsessive compulsive disorder and severe anxiety, we must all become more aware of this serious problem. With research suggesting that over 75% of illnesses are stress related, we need to help our children in ways that do not require earlier prescriptions for medication. And with new fields in epigenetics linking distress from difficult childhoods to problems for future generations, this is not a problem that will simply go away.

Experiencing our feelings

Many of the concern's children may face when coming to you will originate from their natural processes of growth and development. A natural response as they journey towards greater awareness and maturity as they find their own place in the world. But add to that the pressures they feel within any new environment and you can see why some of our children might need a little extra help. With every experience laying the groundwork for the person they are becoming, it is important that you recognise this process and welcome opportunities to embrace their positive feelings. At the same time as knowing if they need some additional support, aware of the early warning signs that they are no longer managing alone.

As I have explored in previous books in this series, when a child continuously feels the same emotion, we might describe this as a mood. In time, continuously feeling this way may lead to a predisposition towards that feeling. We might call this a temperament. And negative temperaments developing as a learned behaviour is something we want to avoid for our children. All feelings are a part of the bodies complex methods of responding to stimulus and protecting itself from any perceived threat, to be able to manage this, children need opportunities to explore their feelings. All of them. But this needs to happen at manageable levels the child can cope with. Simply put, feelings need to be felt, acknowledged and moved on from (Figure 5.1).

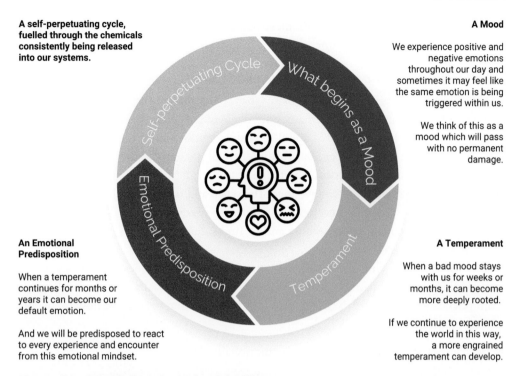

A self-perpetuating cycle, fuelled through the chemicals consistently being released into our systems.

A Mood

We experience positive and negative emotions throughout our day and sometimes it may feel like the same emotion is being triggered within us.

We think of this as a mood which will pass with no permanent damage.

An Emotional Predisposition

When a temperament continues for months or years it can become our default emotion.

And we will be predisposed to react to every experience and encounter from this emotional mindset.

A Temperament

When a bad mood stays with us for weeks or months, it can become more deeply rooted.

If we continue to experience the world in this way, a more engrained temperament can develop.

Figure 5.1: The Thinking and Feeling Cycle – Every time a child experiences strong emotions, chemical receptors respond to manage these within the body. If negative emotions are continuously felt, the body adapts, ready to respond to the expectation of more negativity.

What does it mean to feel anxious?

As children grow and develop, they are learning and experiencing many new things. Their minds and bodies are maturing daily and new situations are being faced and internalised. While for many this is taken in their stride, for others childhood can become fraught with fear and anxiety. As their imaginations grow, for some this can open a world of possibility, for others it can feel like the walls are closing in as their worst fears are continuously considered and anticipated.

Felt at the right level, our fears help us focus on threats and avoid danger by triggering our flight, fight, or fright response. Anxiety, however, is a more persistent, or enduring response to a both real and perceived threat, greater than the situation warrants. It can make us feel sick, nervous, restless or tense as we become highly tuned to our perceptions of danger, panic or dread. At extreme levels or when these feelings are experienced repeatedly, this unhealthy response will get in the way of all the other things a growing child should be experiencing and internalising. They may find themselves trapped within a cycle of prolonged anxiety, or a "learned helplessness" may have established as they resign themselves to feeling this way. They may experience physical symptoms such as headaches or dizziness. And left unchecked, this level of tension within the body can lead to some worrying long-term effects.

What does it mean to a child to feel safe and secure?

A child's emotions can be shown in many shapes and forms. For some children, they may seem happy, only to have their anxieties triggered in different ways and worsen for a range of reasons. It is then only natural to wish to remove any triggers and avoid anxiety altogether for your children, but this intent will not resolve the situation. You are unlikely to remove stress from any child's life entirely, but you can help them to recognise their level of anxiety and to give them the space and techniques they need to manage it. Supporting them to develop self-regulating systems to calm themselves when their emotions become overwhelming and to find stillness and reconnect as they learn to safely navigate this chaotic world.

Fundamental to a child's level of well-being, is the ability to feel safe and secure. At its core, this means similar things to us all at any age and essentially speaks of feeling safe from physical or mental harm. But scratch a little deeper and we can see how these core aspects involve layers of need.

- To feel safe and secure means feeling emotionally safe

- It means being allowed to express yourself without ridicule

- Not being made to feel uncomfortable, vulnerable or alone

- To be allowed to express who you really are rather than conforming to expectations

- Having a sense of control, both of yourself and the environment you are in

- And connected to the other people around you.

These seem like pretty basic requirements but consider these things through the eyes of a child. Who, with developing emotions and behaviours, is attempting to settle within the new environments they now find themselves in. To a child with little control over where they go or what might happen to them when they get there, it can sometimes feel like none of this can be taken for granted. Add to that the stress of needing to perform and measure up in an increasingly fast-paced world, it is then no wonder that levels of anxiety are on the rise.

What does it mean to feel happy?

While we all want our children to be open to happiness, to believe that the good in their lives outweighs the bad, we cannot make our children happy. Even when short-lived interventions may offer to do just that. And yet left unmanaged, high levels of anxiety can have devastating effects over the long-term. So how can you help children find happiness and manage their anxiety before they reach these higher levels of concern?

Figure 5.2: Children find happiness when they are engaged in something with meaning. We cannot always know where they will find this, but we can see the signs when they do.

Research done at the University of Pennsylvania suggested that there were three interlinking aspects of happiness: pleasure, engagement and meaning. These often become merged in real life, so as you think about ways of offering these opportunities for your children in consistent and lasting ways, think beyond the pleasure an experience might bring to consider how engaging it might be or the meaning that it might hold (Figure 5.2).

Happiness can then mean different things to different children. For some it is being with their friends, for others it may be about quietly playing with a favoured toy in peace and solitude. One child may prefer to always be on the go, running, climbing, pushing their bodies and abilities to their newfound limits, while another might be happier discovering new things. Happiness, in terms of pleasure, engagement, and meaning is more than a sign of well-being; it lays the groundwork for other positive outcomes. But it is an emotion, just like anger or fear, and as such no one can determine how you feel it. This is a deeply personal thing. But with guidance and support, we can teach our children ways of creating happiness for themselves. Ways that last longer and are more influential than today's purchase or tomorrow's promise.

Understanding

Understand what anxiety means, what is happening inside the body and the effects this can have in the short and long term

We think of anxiety as a feeling of general unease, perhaps worry or fear that ranges from mild to severe. In its proper place, perhaps when a significant event is approaching, this is perfectly normal. It becomes a problem however when this anxiety becomes uncontrolled, constant or is affecting daily life. By understanding the developmental processes your children are going through and the demands associated with each of these changes, you can learn to support their well-being. And when we share this with the other adults in their lives, we can work together to alleviate some of the anxieties our children may be experiencing.

What happens when we feel anxious?

Anxiety can be experienced in various ways, a racing heart, clammy hands, wobbly legs or a tied feeling in the stomach. It can make us feel sick, nervous, restless or tense as we become highly tuned to our perceptions of danger, panic or dread. While we have all felt these ways at times, imagine feeling this way all the time. This level of tension within the body cannot be sustained without some worrying long-term effects. And all the while a child is feeling this way, they are certainly not focused on any higher order thinking you may be trying to teach them. Like I said, wishing to avoid anxiety altogether for a child is a natural response, but this does not manage the situation either.

When we experience anxiety, the body recognises it as a warning of approaching danger and our defence mechanisms kick in. These primitive responses are the body's automatic reaction to stressful situations, physically stimulating the release of higher levels of adrenaline and cortisol into the bloodstream as it readies the body to deal with the perceived threat. You will recognise the way these hormones feel when they begin surging around your body, your heart beats faster, your breathing quickens and you become hyper alert as your concentration becomes trained on the thing that is threatening you.

If you know a child who is struggling, who seems to feel anxious a lot of the time, you are unlikely to remove stress from their life. But you can help them to recognise their level of anxiety and to give them the space and techniques they need to manage it. And as is the case with many of these things, the earlier you start the better. But first, you need to be aware of any emotions you yourself maybe triggering.

Primitive Brain reactions to modern day problems

When we experience anxiety at healthy levels, this is our body recognising what it considers to be an approaching danger and warning us to get ready for it. What we then feel is our flight, fight or fright response kicking in as we get ready to manage this threat. In these moments it can feel like we are both in the emotion and at the same time, separate from it. Almost as if we are looking down at ourselves. This is because the primitive part of our brain has taken over, where the automatic programmes of *Flight, Fight* and *Fright* reside. And is also why, in these moments, it can feel like we have no control.

If this is a speeding car coming towards you, this system will offer you your best chance of survival. And provided you do not make a habit of stepping into the road without looking, this influx of stress hormones quickly disperses, and the body returns to its previous state. The danger comes when your stress response is repeatedly being triggered or remains triggered for long periods. For a child who is less able to understand what is going on around them, this can be a reality they quickly fall into. Their body then spends too much energy ridding itself of these stress hormones and eventually becomes accustomed to them, existing for long periods in a hypersensitive state.

Whilst this plays an essential role in getting us out of the way of that oncoming car, we do not want to rely on our primitive brain when our best friend has just said something mean about our drawing. However, for children who are immersed in emotions that they do not yet fully understand, upset feelings of anger or hurt can be their often-instant response.

But before we can help anyone else to manage their anxiety, we need to have a handle on our own. Especially when our continued connection with this other person is going to naturally see our emotions transfer to them. Sometimes all it takes is to spend time with someone feeling anxious or excited to begin to physiologically respond in that way too. Recognising their emotions and taking them on as your own. Researchers have seen this effect in children from a very early age. In one study, researchers caused mothers to feel stressed then, when reuniting them with their one-year-old child, noted that the child's heart rates increased to match their mums', even though the children had not been exposed to the stressful situation themselves.

Avoiding your own stress

We are all managing varying levels of stress throughout our day. And despite its promises to ease our lives, the technology we are increasingly surrounded by can leave us with a sense that our control is slipping away. From its instant updates, its increased sensationalism and its demands for instant productivity, to its implication that we must consistently perform and measure up. It is no wonder then that we can often feel the need to stand in the middle of a field and scream... and that is before you add the demands of everyday living into the mix! It is no wonder then that all our levels of anxiety are on the rise.

However, when we feel stressed around our children, they no longer feel at ease and secure in our care. You will see this in their increasingly fraught responses which can serve to increase your own level of stress and potentially that of the others around you as a cycle of stress gathers momentum. Unfortunately, the more stressed you become the less likely you are to deal with any situation in a calm, well considered manor. Instead, you may turn to short-lived highs with a coffee break or a sugary snack as you seek the energy boost you feel yourself needing. However, spiking caffeine and blood sugar levels will only exacerbate the problem and the all-encompassing downward spiral intensifies (Figure 5.3).

As difficult as it can be when you find yourself in these spiralling trajectories of impending despair, try to reflect on these moments after things have calmed down. Take a minute to review what happened and put considered interventions in place to begin easing and in time, avoiding these deeply upsetting times. For me, knowledge and understanding were

Figure 5.3: Taking a moment to understand what is at the root of a child's anxiety will always be the best way to support them in that moment.

always the most effective way of reducing my stress. When I understood my child wouldn't stop crying because her little tummy was tied in knots of colic, it didn't make the crying any quieter, but it did make it easier to understand and manage. Today, realising arguing with a teenager whose brain and thinking processes are as yet structured in quite different ways to my adult one allows me to see the futility of all but the necessary battles! And in just the same way, understanding what is at the root of a child's anxiety can help you to manage the behaviours this may be triggering.

Support

Be supported to implement strategies that guide children toward helping themselves and realising long-term change

As adults, many of us have learnt that to manage life within this chaotic world, we need to find space within ourselves for quiet and relaxation. To ground ourselves within our own states of awareness, in touch with what is occurring on the inside. Whether we do this through hitting the gym, listening to gentle music or walking the dog this process of finding inner calm can help us to feel better about ourselves and more ready to face the things we are less in control of.

Children need no less. When we deny children these opportunities to simply allow the matters of the day to settle, to be calm and still, this places hidden pressures on their body. While this is a practice worth noting for all of us, it is so much more pronounced in a growing child. But you can limit the damage being caused by allowing children these moments of calm within their day, at a time when they have identified a need for it. As you help your children to recognise their emotions and the processes driving their behaviours they can learn to value this time and space before emotions escalate. And the first step towards helping them with this is in knowing what may be triggering their anxiety in the first place.

Helping children to recognise their own anxieties

The first step here is to offer children opportunities to become engaged. As you plan lessons, consider how you will recognise how engaged your children are becoming. Can they find pleasure and meaning in the tasks they are performing? Then, as you help them find these elements throughout the day, be mindful of any early signs of anxiety as it develops and begin to identify the little things you can do to help them.

As you work with a child who might be experiencing increased anxieties, you may be tempted to try and take all their anxieties away. To promise them they will never have to experience anything negative again. But if we always rescue children, they do not learn important coping skills for themselves. Instead, show them the faith you have in their ability to manage these anxieties. Start off small as you encourage small steps around their fear, asking them to suggest ways of managing the situation. Be on hand to support them if they need you, but also be ready to step back and offer them a chance to find the words, to break bigger problems down into the smaller, manageable roots of them. Provided you are always mindful of their capabilities, their sense of achievement under your guidance will do wonders.

We also need to be mindful of the research showing that negative moods tend to narrow a person's focus, whereas a positive mood can increase attention, creativity and flexible thinking. As you look to encourage your children's thinking consider the experiences you are offering with their mood in mind. If you are struggling to support their coping skills and social skills, consider if hidden anxieties could be at the root of the problem. Even five minutes of exercise in the presence of nature can enhance one's mood. But all this needs to begin from their first experiences with you. Once a child has begun to feel invisible, voiceless or that no one cares, this can establish in them a deep-rooted sense of who they are that will stay with them into their teenage years and beyond.

Recognising the triggers

As you look to understand a child's anxieties, try to identify the times and situations that act as stressful triggers to them. Are times of transition, group times, pair work or leaving particular environments typically moments of impending doom? Can you recognise and begin to understand the precise reasons for this? Are you always pushed for time? Are there too many demands on your children causing them to feel panicked? Once you have this understanding you can begin to manage their responses more effectively. Then, work with the child to develop their self-regulating systems as they learn to calm themselves when their emotions become overwhelming. And help them to find ways of returning to a sense of inner peace.

Help children to look at a situation and see what can be altered and that which is beyond their control. Use this to focus their attention, as they consider what to change, while learning to accept the things that they cannot manage. As you do this, be aware of unrealistic expectations. Sometimes fears are rooted in not measuring up to some goal they are not physically or mentally ready for. Instead, foster curiosity and exploration as you help them learn to embrace a challenge. As they see any potential mistakes as simply steps on a journey, they learn to no longer fear them and will be more inclined to grasp future challenges and opportunities.

Voicing the fear

As you help a child to recognise their own triggers of anxiety, start by supporting them to voice their fears. This may need to begin by helping them to find and use their voice in other ways. As they learn to express the thoughts in their head, help them feel like their opinions and ideas are heard and matter. Even if this starts in the smallest of ways by them choosing what you will do today. Then when they are beginning to feel anxious, talk through their anxiety, as you give words to it. As they recognise and begin to name their anxieties, they are no longer a scary, unknown. Instead, you can explore what they really mean. How bad would it be if this happened? How likely is it to happen? Could they or should they do something about it? What steps might they take?

Some children worry that even thinking terrible thoughts will somehow make terrible things happen. If this is the case, ask them to close their eyes and REALLY imagine that there is a giant ice-cream in front of them as they realise that their thoughts alone do not hold the power. For younger children, calling their anxiety a silly name can help them take control of it. For older children, the phrase "I'm having the thought that" in front of what frightens them can help them to gain a different perspective.

Seek to savour

You can help an anxious child to balance their more difficult times with memories of happier, more stable moments. Children do not have a well-developed sense of time and will struggle to imagine a time in the future when they will no longer feel this bad. So, help to bring them back to happier times as you notice and draw attention to the positive experiences in life. Help them anticipate the future and remember times from before, focusing on the positive feelings and experiences you have shared as you exchange positive feelings and experiences as a group.

You can encourage this technique further by practicing tricks of anticipating future events and remembering good ones from before. On the lead up to lunch, talk about how good it will smell and taste, consider how it will feel to sit with their friends. Relive happy memories from a visit you had last week or something funny that happened this morning, using all their senses as you practice these techniques. And as your understanding of your children develops, you can notice when difficult times may be approaching and seek to balance this by reminding them of more stable times (Figure 5.4).

Figure 5.4: Some time alone, moments shared with a friend or being reminded of what's to come can all help manage child anxiety and retain a feeling of calm.

Then offer opportunities to just "be". When they go outdoors encourage them to enjoy the space, to experience the nature all around them as they run and explore. Help them focus on all their senses as you help them to become more mindful of them. But as you begin looking at ways of mediating a child's anxiety, consider where they have this space to relax every day? Where can they go to be free of noise and excessive movement? Are there boundaries or routines you could put in place to safeguard times for quite relaxation? How can a child's voice be heard, even before they have all the words they need? And can they listen to their bodies with the permissions to give it what they need?

When their anxieties are affecting others

Sometimes when we feel anxious, we cannot help but make others around us feel anxious too. Other times anxious behaviours, whether actions or words, may become difficult for other children to manage. If need be, help a child to take a moment as you make sure their own feelings are not overwhelming them, before helping them to consider the feelings of others with a calm and considered response.

Once all the children are calm and can hear what you are saying, you can remind them that sometimes we can all say or do things we do not mean and that their friend looks pretty upset now too. As you help them to find their words and consider the feelings and realities that the other person may be managing, together you can think of a more considered response. Before any real damage is done to the relationship.

And ultimately… look to break the cycle

The more we feel any mood, the more it becomes a part of the character traits we are developing. But when we feel ourselves slipping into a negative mood, it has the added effect of narrowing our focus, causing a sense of isolation that can feel like these difficult emotions are being managed alone. Without timely support, a child may begin to feel invisible, that they are voiceless or that no one cares. And this can establish within them a deep-rooted sense of who they are that will stay with them into their teenage years and beyond.

We cannot always control what happens to us, but we can affect how we respond, especially when we recognise how important it is to do so. So, as you guide and support children to find their own happiness, help them to develop the skills and attitudes to create it within themselves, rather than being fed expectations of happiness from others. Do this and you will be establishing a foundation for positive outcomes and general well-being that will last throughout their lives.

6 Nurturing confidence in the classroom

As we learnt in Chapter 5, anxiety refers to feeling worried, nervous or uneasy about something whose outcome we are uncertain of. But life is unpredictable and full of uncertainties as we face every kind of experience. There are times in all our lives when we need that little bit of extra support, when things feel a little too tough to handle by ourselves and we look for that safe place to return to. But for a child who may not have been with you for very long or who is not used to feeling this way, you need to make sure they know how to find you before they begin to struggle.

Felt at the right level, our fears help us focus on threats and avoid danger by triggering our flight, fight or fright response. But as we learnt in the last chapter, anxiety is a more persistent or enduring response to a both real and perceived threat, greater than the situation warrants. It can make us feel sick, nervous, restless or tense as we become highly tuned to our perceptions of danger, panic or dread. And if it is felt all the time, as can be the case with an unsettled child in a school classroom this level of tension within the body is going to have some worrying long-term effects.

Many things may be causing increased anxiety in a child; conflicts with peers, settling into a new environment, difficulties at home or in school. It could even be a biological issue, such as extended sleep disruption. At extreme levels or when these feelings are experienced repeatedly, this unhealthy response gets in the way of all the other things a growing child should be experiencing and internalising. With repercussions on their social, academic and personal future. Learning to cope with anxiety means learning to manage the uncertainties of life and move forward with courage despite our fears. So rather than seeking to eliminate anxiety, we need to teach our children how to find their courage and to feel confident, with faith in their abilities to do so.

DOI: 10.4324/9781003327059-7

Knowledge

Know the difference between normally fluctuating levels of confidence and emerging anxiety

When research looks to understand the impact of different circumstances on children, it often talks about the long-term effects experienced by a child and their reduced chance of attaining their full potential. Concerned for their ongoing ability to function within society, relationships and other areas of life, these effects are often quantified for the purposes of such studies through higher chances of teenage pregnancy,

Figure 6.1: Early identification of at-risk factors allows strategies to be put in place, allowing you to support a child's self-initiative, self-control and attachments within a nurturing environment.

behavioural issues or mental and physical health problems. But difficult beginnings manifest themselves in ways far deeper and more impactful than these statistics can hope to fully demonstrate (Figure 6.1).

While you may have no influence on the biological or environmental risk factors influencing the children in your classroom, there is much that you can do. Early identification of children at-risk allows strategies to be put in place, both in settings, at school and in the home. Helping to develop the protective factors children need to successfully adapt to risk and adversity in the future. The Devereux Early Childhood Assessment (DECA) is a nationally standardised rating scale designed to evaluate the protective factors associated with resilience and looks at a child's self-initiative, their self-control and attachment. By looking at factors such as these, along with the nature of a child's behaviour and their emotional and social development we can identify the children most at risk and develop intervention plans that can meet their individual needs from an early age.

Why are some children resilient while others struggle?

Many children may encounter high levels of difficulties and stress in their young lives. For some this may have devastating effects that determine their life trajectory for years to come, while others go on to lead happy, highly successful lives. These children are often identified as being resilient; possessing the strength to overcome a difficult beginning and thrive. Many studies have been conducted to understand what makes this difference. Why can some children bounce back while others crumble?

From evidence rooted in the seminal works on child and adolescent resilience of the 1970s, negative outcomes that may have once been considered inevitable are no longer thought of this way. With growing studies showing that such outcomes can, in some circumstances, be circumvented and resilience nurtured. So, if we are looking to enable the potential of all our children, it is then imperative that we understand both the environmental factors that place children at risk and the protective influences that we and other influential adults in their lives can put in place to support them. But first we need to make sure we are aware of what these are.

As we saw in Chapter 5, happiness in terms of pleasure, engagement and meaning is more than a sign of well-being; it lays the groundwork for other positive outcomes. But happiness is an emotion, just like anger or fear. As such no one else can determine how happy or sad we feel, neither can we make others feel any emotion, this is a deeply personal thing. But with our guidance and support, we can teach our children ways of creating happiness for themselves that they can rely on, even in difficult times. Ways that last longer and are more influential than today's purchase or tomorrow's promise.

Whilst we cannot make someone feel anything, continuously feeling the same way about something will ultimately lead to a predisposition towards that feeling. And as we have seen, where negative moods can tend to narrow a person's focus, positive moods can increase their attention, their creativity and flexible thinking. It is then important to your children's social, academic and personal futures that you welcome any opportunity to recognise and embrace their positive feelings. Both in the classroom and out of it. Effectively nurturing their coping skills and fostering healthy responses to all the opportunities around them.

Research at Boston University showed that connecting with an anxious child in an attentive but non demanding way for just five minutes a day had a profound impact. You can replicate these findings by simply gathering a few non-competitive items together, such as crayons, dolls or building blocks and play together for five minutes. As you do so, keep all your attention on the child, rather than conversations with others, any pre-conceived agendas or allowing yourself to become distracted. Then, avoiding asking any questions, correcting or giving any instructions, allow the child to direct the activity.

It is important that they experience this time without tension or worry, as you create a warm and relaxed atmosphere around them. With these memories of spending safe time together, of connecting with you and having you to lean on, you become someone they can trust. Someone who will help them to manage their fears. When this is not in place, a child can feel like they are facing their fears or the more difficult times alone. This is especially important for anxious children who may be struggling to retain any level of confidence a lot of the time and lays the groundwork for when a situation can feel especially bad. However, as with anything like this, have faith in your knowledge of your children. If you are worried about a child, it is probably something to be worried about. Watch out for early signs of difficulty such as physical symptoms manifesting such as headaches or dizziness. Especially if you are noticing prolonged periods of sadness that have come on suddenly, without any obvious explanations. Left unchecked, this may well lead to more severe and ongoing problems.

Developing children's confidence for learning

Unsurprisingly, research suggests that when our children have well-developed social skills, they tend to be more confident, they are more accepted by their peers and actually do better academically. As well as being significantly less susceptible to the difficult school experiences some children find themselves facing. Despite this, evolutionary theorists often talk about survival of the fittest, about an innate level of relentless competition, where you must constantly strive to remain on top. You may recognise this within your own experiences of your school days, with league tables, posted grades and Head Boy or Head Girl, where getting noticed and recognised depends on individual actions and achievements, rather than putting others first. But this is not the way we are genetically predisposed to live. We would not have survived as a species if we had not nurtured the social skills that allow us to support one another (Figure 6.2).

Figure 6.2: From their earliest experiences of working together, children are learning what it means to be part of a team, to have ideas and respond to others.

Developing the social skills required to work with others is then an important life skill. Whether in the business world, academia or in social situations. Co-operating with others is necessary for our general well-being, as well as instrumental within achieving many of our goals. Within the school classroom, children are often asked to work together, either in pairs or small groups and often with the child they would not have selected. Some are better at this than others, but evidence suggests that this social skill can be taught and improved with practice as we gain experience within these social interactions.

As children develop the skills to understand and manage their emotions, they become more confident and better able to show what they can do in the classroom. They learn to cooperate and work together, building stronger connections with their peers and are better able to navigate any conflicts as they arise. They are also more aware of the demands asked of them and the actions they need to take to see them through. All of which have both immediate and lifelong benefits.

Understanding

Understand the effects of anxiety on a developing child's body when it goes unchecked

Children are born with tremendous optimism and ability to bounce back. But this optimism naturally drops during childhood as they become more self-aware and self-critical. If this is not managed during childhood, our teenagers can become deeply disillusioned, with the world and their place in it. They can become lost in depression and other forms of mental illness or hide in alcohol and drug abuse, an increasing problem as these substances have become more widely available. It is then so important that during these formative years, you look to identify the triggers surrounding a child's increased anxiety and consider how you can address them. Can you ease over-lapping demands or unrealistic expectations? Can you organise your time more sympathetically? Can you create a more relaxing environment where they feel more safe and secure?

Feeling anxious

Whenever we experience a particularly emotional event, thought chemicals are released into the body to inform us of our response to it. As we experience the world, or even think about it, the neurons in our brain release these chemicals to trigger reactions in the body that we feel as emotions. Anything from a slight flutter felt in the tummy, to a debilitating physical reaction. Happy and empowering thoughts produce chemicals to make us feel happy and empowered. Whilst negative, sad or angry thoughts produce chemicals that make us feel sad, angry or depressed. When in a healthy balance, these processes inform our responses and empower our reactions. However, trouble soon comes when they are unmatched to our need for them.

Take fear for example. That feeling of a racing heart and rapid breathing as the body is flooded with oxygen, preparing its flight, fight or fright response to the danger it perceives, readying it for action. A healthy reaction when that perception of fear is accurate, but heightened levels of fear or anxiety long before an active response is needed is not a healthy state to be in. Think back to the last time you had to wait weeks for a test result. Or imagine eagerly awaiting a holiday but needing to board a plane when you are petrified of flying.

If a child is consistently experiencing the world in a particularly emotional way, predispositions to those emotions can develop. Having emotions connected with certain times of the day, can establish patterns of responses long before they are needed. Such as dread around particular activities or anxiety over transitioning into a different environment for example. These events can be long anticipated with harmful effects on a child's body and overall quality of life. And to make matters worse, children do not have a well-established sense of time. They are less aware of how long they have to wait for these events to happen and they may struggle to imagine a time when they will not feel this bad.

Keeping lines of communication open

Before a child can begin to manage themselves through the more difficult times of uncertainty, they need to have established a sense of safety and security. The best thing you can do for your children is then to ensure they have secure attachments to the caring adults around them. By establishing this groundwork, their sense of well-being can flourish as they learn to handle the more demanding times, to take risks and weather the unpredictability's that lie ahead.

In Chapter 2 we considered ways in which you can communicate with your children, playing with them, engaging with them and making the connections that allow these deep-rooted attachments to occur. As you find ways in which to communicate as you play and interact, you are engaging with them and making the connections that allow the deep-rooted attachments children still need to occur. This will not be the same for every child, nor indeed for every day. You will then need a varied tool kit at your disposal. But through these nondemanding exchanges, you are laying the groundwork that is so important to a child. Establishing a sense of security, as well as offering a safe harbour for them to return to, whenever things get tough.

Once these foundations are in place, you have then taken massive strides forward in helping a child to manage their anxieties before they become a crisis. Firstly, because you will be more aware of any changes that are suggesting things are becoming more difficult. And secondly, because you will be ready to act, with underpinning coping mechanisms that you have put in place and that they have learnt to trust in.

Do your children have a safe harbour to return to when things get stormy?

Known in psychology as social referencing, children will look to a person they trust to take their cues, secure in the knowledge that you are there for them and ready to catch if they stumble. If this is not in place, a child will feel like they are facing these more difficult times alone. If they are already anxious, they will simply learn to avoid anything connected to that anxiety and while this may offer some immediate and temporary relief, it can see anxiety in these areas grow. So, remain connected to your children as you help them manage and move past their fears with compassion and gentle encouragement. And be really mindful of the messages you are giving to them.

For example, what would your reaction be if children were keen to go hunting for the bugs you are learning about outside? If they then run to you, eager to show you the large hairy spider they have found, they will look to you to see how you respond, learning from your reaction. If you are relaxed, they are more likely to be. If you react with increased emotions, their potential anxiety around spiders will be growing in preparation for the next encounter with an eight-legged friend, especially if anxiety is becoming a default reaction for them (Figure 6.3).

Figure 6.3: The way you respond to the things that are important to a child sends many messages about how they should respond. Are the bugs on my leaf fascinating or something I should be anxious about?

You do not need to look to avoid anxiety in these moments or deny that it exists or even look to belittle its power. Instead, help each other to be brave together, doing something even though you may be afraid of it. If you feel nervous around spiders, use this as an opportunity to face your fears together. Talk about what it is you do not like, explore with them how sometimes our fears may be irrational. You know the spider cannot hurt you, but you feel frightened anyway. And help them to see that there may be things they feel braver about than you do, helping their confidence to grow.

Through these exchanges you are getting to know you children very well. And for that anxious child, you can be ready to recognise when things are becoming too much for them to handle. Remember, if there is something to be worried about, your children need you to know them on a deep enough level to be able to pick up on this. So, take the time to really connect with your children and build the safe harbours they know they can always return to. And if you are working with a child who seems to have been struggling for what seems like weeks, it may be time to consider professional intervention. Especially if you feel like prolonged periods of difficult emotions have come on suddenly or without any obvious explanations.

Support

Be supported with steps you can take to encourage a child's confidence, to recognise anxiety within themselves and to give them back a sense of confidence and control

A child's confidence in the classroom may depend on a range of things, as unique as each child and situation you encounter. However, at the root of this confidence and the anxieties that may be triggered in its absence there are some familiar sounding issues. As we have seen in the last few chapters, for a child to feel confident, they need to have trust in themselves. They need to have experienced the things they are able to do, with an empowering belief that when they encounter a new challenge, that this too can be tackled.

Acknowledge a child's anxiety

There will of course be times when every child faces a level of anxiety or a moment of self-doubt. You can begin to manage these moments by helping children to feel the natural responses of their body and to not be afraid of them. Just like if you ask them to run around the playground their breathing will quicken, their hearts will beat faster and they may feel a little sweaty. This is simply their body responding to the task at hand as they use their muscles in different ways.

When they begin to feel anxious, this is simply their body sensing something that in this moment it perceives as a threat. Whilst this reaction may be a little too strong for the situation, their body is following a natural process of trying to keep them safe and is getting their body ready to run away from it, either physically or mentally. Help them to understand that these feelings cannot be maintained for very long. And remind them that, even when they are in the middle of an anxiety attack, these feelings will pass as you help them to find the words to tell you how they feel. They may again talk about racing hearts, rapid breathing or sweaty palms. Guide them toward seeing that these reactions are again a natural response to something their body needs to do, it is just that this time it may need a little support to get it just right.

Give them the space and opportunity to find who they are

To foster confidence in your children, you need to give them an opportunity to try. You need to be ready to acknowledge their success with targeted praise and to help them see challenge as simply a part of the learning process. You need to establish a learning environment where children feel enabled to try things for themselves. And to access the resources, experiences and guidance they need to take the next step. Essentially preparing children for a diverse and ever-changing world, in ways that simply conforming in recognised and expected ways never can.

The trouble is, if we become too focused on the agenda and outcomes of the day, we can overlook the importance of a child's confidence within the classroom. And instead, look to value the conforming "on-task" child who appears to be disciplined and well suited to the environment. What this really means is that they can sit still for long periods of time and listen to the thoughts and knowledge of the teacher. As children's efforts become focused on working hard to do what the teacher expects of them, ask yourself, is this really stimulating our next generation of thinkers and problem solvers? Does this really equip them with the skills they need to make meaning of their own lives, to recognise what is good and what needs to change? To embrace a social awareness and enable great things to happen?

Help children find their own opportunities for purposeful involvement

If we undervalue a child's need for choice and independence, we are suggesting that their autonomy needs little acknowledgement. However, removing anyone's feeling of control can spin us all into feelings of anxiety. Children then need a level of autonomy that allows them to find relevance and a place for their actions and efforts.

Children are individuals and they need opportunities to approach things in their own way. This may not be the same as others in the class or indeed how it was yesterday. But if we overlook these individual needs, anxiety levels will rise. If we view our role as giving children the facts they need to pass a qualification, what about the other possible ways of doing and being that could open our world to so much? If we view children through an assessment lens with test-based accountability, we compare them to a version of themselves that we want them to live up to. If conformity is valued and planned for, more than a child's investigations and experimentations, what depths of possibility are we missing out on? And then we wonder why our children are feeling anxious.

■ Education needs to offer children all they need to be all they can be

■ We need to view their ideas and interests with as much significance as our own

■ Children need to receive the same level of respect within what is their learning environment as anyone else

■ To do otherwise grossly underestimates their ability

■ And as a direct result, their confidence in their own ability.

Give children a voice

Let children have a say in what they are interested in and the directions they want to follow. Even by giving them a say in the rules of the classroom allows for a sense of belonging and control that eases anxiety (Figure 6.4).

Help children to see the good in all they do

As I discuss in Chapter 8 and through the other books in this series, the key here is to offer praise and encouragement for the positive things that children are in control of. So, not how clever or great they are, but how hard they have worked at something or the ongoing effort they have shown a difficult task.

Figure 6.4: From their first experiences of it, children need to feel they are a valued member of the classroom community with a voice that means something.

Verbally notice the good you see

When you make a point of acknowledging something positive, not only are you drawing a child's attention to it, but you are also letting them know that you are paying attention and that they are worthy of your attention. This does not need to be a grand gesture or in fact be heard by anyone else. For some children a quite word or smile from across the room is more readily accepted and valued.

Allow children to set their own targets

When children are given this opportunity they can concentrate their focus on the things that are important to them. They can recognise the small wins, while you help this process to remain as individual as your unique children are.

Allow children to express their fears

Sometimes the worst feature of a problem is the magnitude it reaches within our own heads. Spoken out loud and the issue can become more manageable. Especially with the understanding and rational outlook of a more experienced adult to support. Remember, children do not have a great understanding of time and will struggle with the concept of a time in the future when things will feel less of a struggle. Neither do they have as many experiences as you may of positive resolutions. You can then help support them with these key triggers to their anxiety.

Allow them to put their mistakes in perspective

No one is perfect but to an anxious child, errors can feel like the end of the world. Help to create a growth mindset where errors are not viewed as something negative. Instead, they are embraced as a natural and empowering part of the learning process. You can encourage this by rephrasing comments such as "I can't" or "I don't know", to "I can't yet" or "I know how to find out".

Offer children a degree of ownership within their day

Think about the decisions or options you can offer the children. While it is tempting to have control of all variables, it is far more empowering to your children to allow for a different way forward. You could have "must do" and "may do" tasks for the day as they explore their own interests or order of what they feel like working on next. This greater sense of control comes hand in hand with a greater sense of achievement as they see a more direct effect of their efforts.

See all your children as the unique individuals they are

Working in a busy classroom it can become easy to think of the girls or the boys, the summer born or the "Green Group". But every one of your children comes to you with their own unique set of experiences, strengths and needs. As you take positive notice of them, they can see the positive qualities in themselves and each other as their confidence blooms.

7 Friendships, conflict and playground dramas

As you will be well aware if you have ever spent time with young children or indeed remember being one yourself, friendships to a child are tremendously important. Their social world will depend on both their one-on-one friendships as well as their social standing within their wider peer group. It will inform who they can sit next to, the conversations they can take part in, the games they are allowed to join and the roles they can take within them as alliances are formed, broken and reformed by the minute. In the early days, while we are still learning how to make, manage and nurture our friendships, the dynamics can change very quickly and altercations tend to be short-lived.

As they get a little older however, children are becoming increasingly aware of how other children view them as the importance of belonging and their status within the group become increasingly important. As do concerns regarding their popularity and fear of rejection. Without the experience and more mature responses needed to manage these situations as well as they will in future years, the issues that arise will be more acutely felt as things get worked out. Arguments, even physical altercations are all a normal part of this process as children develop more mature social skills. In fact, studies have shown that children in the playground can engage in ordinary meanness on average every 2–3 minutes, physical aggression may occur every 10 minutes and verbal attacks every 30 minutes. It is then inevitable that at some point, every child will be mean to someone else and they in turn will do or say something mean back.

As hard as it may be when children are becoming upset, it is important to remember that this is a natural part of childhood and the development of our more mature social skills. You need to be sympathetic, but offer gentle confidence that with appropriate support, they will be able to manage the situation. Even if this requires some guidance in the beginning. In this way, ordinary conflict is less likely to escalate into more difficult issues that will set patterns for the next encounter. As you model caring and considerate interactions yourself, reassure your children of the warm, supportive communities

DOI: 10.4324/9781003327059-8

they are a part of. And look to inspire the behaviours that will not only attract genuine friendships, but also minimise the negative effects of any difficult behaviours children may experience.

Knowledge

Know what normal friendship dilemmas and disputes look like between young children and when these might need a level of adult intervention

While all children's emotions are going to be dependent on their state of mind and how they are feeling in the moment, children are also getting older. Their emotions are maturing, along with their methods of experiencing and displaying them. These emotions are also becoming increasingly informed by the emotional dispositions that are developing within them. These pre-established influences on their emotional behaviours are a result of their genes, as well as all their previous experiences. It is then so important that we value every opportunity we are given to mould positive responses to even the most difficult emotions.

Research at the University of Minnesota looked at the social struggles occurring at the beginning of every school year, noting as a "dominance" and hierarchy within the year groups established. Within every engagement, one child would notch up a "win", while another would "lose" as others in the classroom looked on with great interest as a social hierarchy network established within the class. Data analysed from these observations have shown that these networks established early on remain remarkably stable from the beginning of the school year to the end, even though the level of challenges quickly drops off after a few weeks. They also found that children who were at the bottom of this dominance hierarchy were more susceptible to bullying behaviours and that the best way to avoid this was through the development of social and emotional skills.

Children's developing emotions

By the time children are around four or five years old, their emotions have become more socially developed. Moving on from relying on adults to balance their emotional state, they are now looking more to their peers as they learn to manage their emotions and solve their own problems. They will now be experiencing mixed emotions, such as being angry and sad at the same time and will begin to use their emotions as unconscious defence mechanisms.

Along with this maturity comes the ability to have simple conversations about their feelings and with guidance, they can learn alternative coping methods when a situation causes their emotions to rise. By the time they are ready for school, children can think about and discuss their emotions in increasingly sophisticated ways. This then allows them to use cognitive coping strategies, such as distraction or self-talk, to think through their emotions and calm themselves. But this also means they are becoming better at hiding their feelings. Whilst this can be a good thing within a social interaction, it also means that you may need to look more closely at their behaviours to see the emotions that they may be masking.

Allowing children to feel their emotions

It is very tempting to shy away from dealing with difficult emotional situations, but it is our job to teach our children how to handle their emotions in healthy ways. No one ever said a furious group of 7-year-olds distraught about the turn a game has taken is easy, but that is exactly when they are ready to learn about how to calm themselves down from anger and how to manage it.

By allowing children to experience their emotions, even the negative ones, they can learn to identify, understand and manage them. And the difficulties that can be experienced when difficult emotions are felt can be better handled. But a child's depth of skill at handling these situations depends on their ability to monitor both their own and other people's emotions, to understand and label the different emotions being shown and to use emotional information to guide their thinking and their behaviours towards them. But often, the physical disputes are the easiest ones to handle. They are certainly more likely to be noticed. So, what about conflict of the more verbal kind?

Prevention as your first line of defence

Emotional meltdowns are often the result of feeling overly hungry, tired, frustrated or simply poorly, especially when their age and developmental stage means the demands and expectations that are being put on them are unrealistic. Prevention is then often the best management tool for what might be dramatic emotional outbursts. So, be aware of a child's triggers and avoid being "past the point of no return" more than you must. And if this is occurring regularly, think about what you are expecting of your children as you consider ways of easing a situation back from the brink.

When you do feel the emotional tensions beginning to rise, look to remain calm and unemotional yourself, as difficult as that may be. You cannot hope to manage a child's heightened emotions if you yourself are beginning to feel overwhelmed, anxious or upset by the situation. Now they are getting a little older, help them to recognise the feelings they are experiencing without being afraid of their emotions or the behaviours they may evoke. Talk to them in calm tones as you look to break the negative behavioural cycles that would otherwise form and instead, reinforce different pathways in their brain. Help them to recognise that this is simply a chemical response surging through their body, causing these feelings but that THEY can decide how to react to them (Figure 7.1).

"I thought she was my friend, but she told on me!"

The research is in... girls and boys "tattle" or "tell tales" on one another equally as often as each other, at least according to a study by Queens University, Belfast. Typically at least once, but sometimes averaging more than six times per day. And the reason... it works! In this study, 70% of the tattles elicited acknowledgement or support from an adult, with only 6% seeing a reprimand

Figure 7.1: The first step in managing dramatic emotional outbursts is to have well established attachments with your children, knowing their potential triggers and being ready to respond to them.

for the tattler. It can also serve as an intermediate step in emotion regulation. Whilst a child may have enough self-control not to hit their frustrating classmate, the ability to effectively negotiate their way out of a situation is not yet within their grasp. Telling tales is then a way for a child to feel like they have managed the situation, that they have been heard and that an adult has understood their concerns.

"Guess what he did...!"

Research demonstrates that gossip is extremely common, making up about two-thirds of naturally occurring conversations. Everyone does it, men, women, young and old. And although content can at times be questionable, it is thought to serve an important social function, creating intimacy within a group and even fuelling reputations. One study that recorded ten-year-old girls for 15-minutes captured 36 instances of gossip, involving 25 different people. However, these kinds of interactions are rarely malicious. Comments are more likely to convey information, "Did you see what she did!" with only 7% tending to indulge in aggressive remarks that could damage reputations or relationships. That is not to say that these kinds of exchanges cannot cause damage and children need to understand that reputations and friendships can be difficult to repair or quickly ruined. Children must also be cautioned of the danger of inventing stories or enhancing malicious details for effect.

So, with all that development of social skills and classroom dynamics, how do we distinguish ordinary acts of meanness and social learning from bullying which is a serious and complicated problem with potentially devastating outcomes?

What is bullying and what can we do about it?

Being the target of bullying is a frightening prospect at any age. It can lead to anxiety, depression or poor self-esteem with effects lasting into adulthood. With long-term consequences that can often be as bad or even worse for the bullies. But to understand bullying, we must first distinguish it from ordinary meanness. While one is a natural part of children finding their way within complicated relationships, bullying is a significant method of peer abuse. A complicated issue, it is one that must be acknowledged and actively managed if we are going to safeguard our children from the devastating effects of it.

Understanding

Understand the negative words and actions that can have ongoing harmful effect

Young children are undergoing complex processes as they learn how to socially engage and interact. They will be experimenting with different responses and reacting from an immature and inexperienced point of reference. Mean things will be said and done and mistakes will be made. All of which can be difficult for them to understand, regardless of the role they may have played within it. A role which also may be changing on a daily basis. Bullying however is something quite different.

Bullying is typically characterised as an abuse of power. Victims of bullying behaviour are typically targeted by virtue of their age, size or perceived weakness. It can also be directed towards those in a weaker position within the group or social standing. But it manifests through the targeting of a particular individual, repeatedly over time through deliberate hurtful or frightening acts. This can take the form of physical, verbal, emotional or cyber abuse. And may use aggressive, terrorising, intimidating, tormenting or shunning tactics. Bullying behaviours cannot be ignored, they are unlikely to "sort themselves out" and are not "a natural part of growing up". In fact, left unmanaged they can do lasting and serious damage to all involved.

Managing low level teasing

Now we know a little about what bullying is and what it is not, it is important that we try to understand it on a deeper level. Most children will, at some point, be teased about something and it can be difficult to know how to support a child who is becoming upset by these social interactions. Research suggests that those children who show the biggest emotional reaction do tend to be the ones that end up targeted more often. You can then help a child who may be falling into these behavioural patterns by showing them ways to avoid more emotional responses when they feel provoked. You can teach them some more generic comebacks to be used in the heat of the moment.

Phrases such as "So what?", "Thanks for noticing!" or "Whatever!" will all do the job and feel enormously empowering for a child who may otherwise feel powerless.

Boys and girls do tend to behave differently when it comes to social conflicts. Where boys tend to turn to physical aggression more quickly, girls will tend to attack the relationship, spreading rumours or excluding someone from the group. With the high value girls place on their intimate friendships, this can be particularly upsetting and its affects should not be underestimated. However, it becomes bullying when manipulation or power is being used, such as those who used to be friends now actively urging others to reject one particular child. And while this may feel incredibly difficult in the moment, often the best option in the immediate term is to support children as they establish more than one circle of friends (Figure 7.2).

Figure 7.2: Friendships, developed over shared interests and moments together are important at every age.

Dealing with playground conflict

When a child has been the target of meanness or conflict, the first thing to do is then to try to understand exactly what happened. This may not come from the children who have been directly involved as they may be more focused on the wrong that was done to them, rather than recognising their own contribution to the problem. In these moments you can offer children strategies to avoid the repeated pattern of difficult behaviours and offer them ways they can cope with it should it happen again.

Being around other children can help, as can playing near an adult. These can be useful strategies while the child is developing their confidence or the social skills to join the play of other groups. Practicing some generic responses ready for any further malicious words or actions may also help. Even if they are never used, having them ready can again offer a child the support they need to bolster their confidence. If you believe there is a case of true bullying occurring, refer immediately to your anti-bullying policy. If these behaviours are ongoing or if there is a real power difference in place, following this policy will be an essential part of ensuring that all children are kept safe. But as you do so, be sure to do so with tact and refer your concerns directly to avoid escalating the problem further.

Cyberbullying

In this increasingly digital age, with greater access to social media and its perceived anonymity, cyberbullying is increasingly becoming a bullying weapon of choice. This may include sending malicious emails or text messages, posting humiliating photos or posting embarrassing information. Although it is less common than real-life bullying, cyberbullying is highly public and easily spread and as a result can be devastating. It is also often faceless, causing additional mental anguish as the attacker and possibly the cause of the attack remains unknown. Cyberbullying may also have a sexual theme that children are vastly unprepared for or mature enough to handle. For example, being pressured into showing intimate body parts, or posting videos of themselves.

Helping children to understand bullying behaviours

Psychologists have found that children often label a bully as someone that is always mean. If bullying behaviours have been interspersed with acts of kindness, a child may not recognise that they are being bullied. Or that their behaviours are in fact, bullying. They may look to explain away the significance of their actions or the actions of others, minimising how bad it is. They may try to compare it to worse behaviour or try to blame the child on the receiving end.

Some children may be used to lying, cheating, arguing and manipulating to get what they want or need in other environments. Having experienced these cycles of behaviour that may have been necessary or have, unfortunately, worked they will need guidance and support to reframe their natural responses. We must then firstly look to identify the rationalisations that are being used with the child. You can then help them to name the emotions that are being felt on both sides, along with the behaviours that are being triggered and the consequences of them. You can then work with the child as you teach them active management of their behaviours. As you do so, be ready to react to any tendencies towards aggression by noticing the early signs of anger when it is easier to calm down. Along with supporting their methods of communicating in assertive rather than aggressive ways (Figure 7.3).

Understanding the child who is doing the bullying

Finding out that a child has been a bully can be deeply troubling and difficult to deal with. However, these behaviours, whilst difficult to deal with on their own, may also be masking other issues that a child may be crying out for your help with. It is then of great importance that you act immediately and decisively. Look to understand the whole issue and remember, behaviours are a child's most powerful method of communication, even the negative ones.

So firstly, do not be tempted to avoid the situation, in doing so you are simply sending a clear message that you are not interested, these behaviours are condoned or that nothing more could be expected of the child who is behaving in these ways. But you are also not looking to seek punishment which does little to address the causes of the

Figure 7.3: The complex and changing dynamics of friendships are continually being experienced in the school playground.

behaviour and if anything reinforces the bullying behaviours. As these identities then become fixed, any aggression is fed off of and bullying behaviours may simply become sneakier.

Your language in all your dealings is deeply influential in these moments. Anything perceived as criticism will instinctively cause a child to justify and defend their actions. Phrases such as "I'm sure you didn't intend to", "I realise it was an accident" or "I'm sure you didn't realise" can be more helpful than other alternatives. You can then follow this up with "What could you do now to help your friend feel better?" or "What plan can we come up with to make sure this doesn't happen again?" As you indicate a belief in their good intentions you can consider their behaviours in the following ways.

Are they seeking to dominate or show power?

If you think this is at the root of their behaviours, help them to see things from another persons perspective. Look back at the chapters on nurturing empathy as they realise the pain they are inflicting is no different to the pain they themselves have felt when upset, frustrated or tormented. If they are looking to show dominance through thinly disguised rough play, engage them in more constructive, energising activities. For example, showing their power and dominance over the climbing of a wall as they do battle with themselves, rather than overcoming another child.

Are they using force or intimidation to get something they want?

They may be overly centred on their own needs, using others to achieve their own goals. Show a child who is using these manipulative tactics some non-aggressive and peaceful ways to negotiate for what they want. You can help them see how their methods are making matters worse, not better. And be particularly mindful of any siblings or peers that have become affected by their actions.

Are they acting out to get noticed?

If a child has been acting out in a bid to be noticed, create opportunities for them to be noticed for the good they can achieve. Rather than simply dictating what they cannot do. Organise opportunities to engage in helpful actions, noticing and caring about the rights and needs of others as they develop a deeper understanding of empathy and sympathy. Especially if this can offer some reparations as they see the consequences of their actions.

Are they re-enacting behaviours from TV viewing and game play?

This one can be controversial. However, studies do repeatedly show that these activities can desensitise children to real-life violence. While other children can become intimidated by the experience, seeing the world as an unsafe and violent place. Closely monitor conversations about computer and TV programming and look out for it being referenced in their play. And remember, violence can be included where you would least expect it, no matter how "intended for children" you think programming might be.

Support

Be supported in recognising the possible causes of conflict as you support children to develop their social skills and friendships while maintaining everyone's happiness

The first step in responding to any child involved in a bullying situation is then to respond to their fears and concerns. Making it clear that they will be listened to, that nothing is too silly or too ugly to be talked about and that their concerns will be received with love and respect, support and encouragement. And if they have found themselves in any destructive or damaging relationships, help them to gain distance from them.

While you talk to your children about the things that were said and done and the feelings that may have prompted an outburst, remember that imagining the feelings of another person is a skill that develops gradually throughout childhood. For a child to respond in a compassionate way is then something that takes a great deal of nurturing experiences and is a behaviour that you can only expect once a child has lost the egocentric motivations of their younger years. This takes active development and practice to do well and unless a child's well-being has been effectively nurtured, they are unlikely to offer a considered or empathetic response to anyone.

However, through your non-judgmental interactions, you can show your children how they can experience their feelings and express their ideas while respecting and accepting the needs and wants of others. You can acknowledge how the other persons behaviours might be displaying an emotion they are feeling, while gently reminding the child in question, that their emotions are all their own. That while the other child may have done something that has resulted in them getting angry, what they choose to do with their anger is a decision that belongs entirely to them.

What if they don't tell me?

Children often resist telling anyone they are experiencing bullying behaviours so, unless there are obvious signs, you might never know. While evidence of physical bullying can be obvious, there are other indicators to be aware of if you suspect a child in your care is having problems.

- A sudden lack of interest in school or particular activities

- Refusing to go to school or to other clubs

- A drop in grades

- Withdrawing from family and school activities, wanting to be left alone

- Conversations or explanations for things that do not quite "ring true"

- Using derogatory or demeaning language when talking about others

- Not talking about their friends or everyday activities.

The unfortunate reality is that difficult behaviours, to some level, are a common occurrence within many childhood experiences. That does not mean that bullying can ever be simply accepted or condoned. Bullying can have devastating consequences on all involved, with the most serious of outcomes. It needs discussing, identifying and managing. But do not wait until you suspect a problem to engage with these discussions with your children. Talk about behaviours that are ok and those that are not, consider the issues you find in books, television or film. And most importantly, demonstrate to your children that they have people they can talk to, no matter what the issue may be (Figure 7.4).

Avoiding being a target for difficult behaviours

Studies show that the best way for a child to avoid negative behaviours is to have a best friend. Simply standing next to a friend will make a child less of a target and having different groups of friends offers more social options and minimises the emotional

Figure 7.4: Talking with children about behaviours and emotions gives them the vocabulary they need and lets them know that they have a safe space to talk whenever they may need to.

impact during difficult times. Children finding themselves at the bottom of the inevitable class hierarchy are naturally more susceptible, so help all children to develop their social skills and offer opportunities to make close friends throughout the different parings and activities you offer. Help children to understand their emotions as you work with them to deal with strong feelings and navigate conflicts. And help them to actively manage their responses as they learn to cultivate their friendships with immediate and lifetime benefits.

- Allow children to choose their own social groupings

- Offer activities for children to come together in different pairs and small groups

- Introduce resources or problems for children to solve that they cannot do alone, such as moving a heavy or cumbersome object

- Avoid breaking up "together time" when you can help it, children need time to engage with one another.

So how do you support a child who is showing bullying tendencies

It can be very difficult to know how to manage an incident of bullying. Especially when it comes to the child doing the bullying. Firstly, you need to recognise that bullying is a form of behaviour and as with any other behaviour, it is a response to feelings and emotions. However, in this case a child's behaviours are having a negative effect on others and must be addressed. This might be in response to stressors in the home; harsh parenting styles, intense arguments or major family problems, all of which can see a confused or angry child act out towards others. It may also be as a result of a sudden or dramatic change that the child is struggling to come to terms with, such as a house move, a change in a parents job, the birth of a sibling or death of a grandparent.

Psychologists talk of two main forms of aggression. Emotionally driven reactive aggression, seen when a frustrated child lashes out. And the cooler proactive aggression, calculated to achieve social power. Reactive aggression tends to be an emotive response as angry children use this as an appropriate and effective way to deal with problems, reacting through impulse rather than cruelty. Proactive aggression uses manipulative methods used to enhance their social dominance, often becoming the most aggressive children on the playground through methods that can be more difficult to address.

- Ensure all children have a voice and a place to use it

- Do everything you can to avoid negative assumptions being made about a child, even by them

- If a child is experiencing difficulties, understand where they are coming from as you look to offer the support and guidance they may need.

Countering Cyberbullying: "Stop, Block, and Tell"

Of course, not all bullying is done face to face. Cyber bullying, for reasons I have mentioned, is an increasingly familiar reality for many young children. The first thing you need to make sure that every child understands is that digital communication comes with absolutely no privacy. Any electronic message or image can be captured and shared to live forever online. So, when talking to children about what they post, ask them to always consider whether they would be happy for their post to be broadcast throughout the school and amongst their family before sending it.

If they ever do encounter cyberbullying, make sure they understand specific instructions about what to do. "Stop, Block, and Tell" is a handy mantra to embrace and display. "Stop" before reacting, "Block" any further messages and "Tell" a trusted adult, who will help them rather than simply taking away access to their devices, which will just make them reluctant to tell you. As with any form of bullying, talk to your children about the specific kinds of behaviours that are not acceptable online. For example, forwarding bullying messages, pretending to be someone else or spreading malicious rumours.

- Display the "Stop, Block, and Tell" mantra, but also talk with children about what this means

- Offer them a safe place to discuss any concerns they may be having

- Ensure these messages are echoed at home.

Taking things further

If you suspect any child is experiencing bullying behaviours of any kind or at any level, ensure you have familiarised yourself with the anti-bullying policies and procedures you have in place and seek support from your designated lead. Detailed notes about your specific concerns will support these discussions, then follow up in the days following asking how the situation is being dealt with. A zero-tolerance policy is not enough. This speaks of punishing the guilty, when things are rarely that simple. A child who has resorted to bullying tactics needs understanding and support as they deal with underlying issues, not punishment. Steps need to be taken to teach children how to manage their anger or misplaced feelings. Punishment seeks only to mask them, often making the situation far worse.

- Ensure everyone is aware of the policy, but also that it is fit for purpose. "We did everything it told us to" is no comfort if a child falls through the gaps

- Reflect on the needs and support of all children in these situations. There is never a place for punishment, children act out for a reason

- Make sure that all conversations are handled with the appropriate training in place. Substantial damage can be done by saying too much, too little or the wrong thing.

8 Developing nurturing methods of encouragement and self-motivation

Throughout their early childhood, children will have undergone a dramatic period of mental growth and development, from the baby they were a few years ago to the school child you see in front of you. To support this, children are born curious and full of a sense of adventure, easily excited and internally motivated as they are driven to form more than 200 trillion brain cell connections or synapses, mapping out the structure and workings of their developing brain. With around 80% of their basic brain architecture now in place, their social and emotional structures are well established, readying each child as they embark on the next stage of their journey and the evolving experiences still to come. Wherever that may take them. These connections have all been dependent on every experience and opportunity that each child has been afforded, meaning that every child is entirely unique with personal views and ways of understanding.

It is then somewhat of a fool's errand to expect every child to react in the same way to any experience that we may offer them, to need the same things from it or to progress through it at the same rate. And yet, an over-reliance on whole class teaching can, for some young children, be an overly common experience. This is not an efficient way of learning and for many, is quite detrimental in the long term. Children often find the pace too fast or too slow and they may become distracted, disengaging from activities that are either too easy, too hard or too repetitive. To help children stay motivated we may then find ourselves showering them with praise, motivations or rewards, even when we don't realise we are doing it. But is this the right thing to do, or teaching them to question any action with "Do I have to do this?", "Does it count?" or "What am I going to get from you if I do?"

Children need experiences that they are personally interested in, with challenges that match their abilities and developmental stage. They need encouragement, feedback and self-discipline to stay self-motivated in ways that they can achieve all the goals that are important to them – and you. And they need to be offered the time and support they

DOI: 10.4324/9781003327059-9

require to develop their understanding before moving on. To do otherwise risks deeply unfulfilling learning experiences, that then lead to a greater reluctance to engage next time. As a vicious cycle establishes, their achievements, as well as their belief in themselves as a learner, can be affected. Along with any motivation to apply the necessary effort going forward. So with all this said, let us consider, how motivated are your children to learn?

Knowledge

Know how and when children are most likely to feel motivated and how you can encourage this

So, what does it mean for a child to be motivated? Motivation is rooted in the belief that your actions are going to result in you achieving the goal you have in mind. Unfortunately, once you start doubting that your actions are likely to have that kind of potential, you are unlikely to keep trying. And if we surround our children with routines, rules and expectations, with little or no power to influence events within their lives, they are unlikely to set their own goals or attempt to achieve them. If this continues, they may simply become content with any situation their life puts them in. If this is a toxic relationship, they may be unable to find their way out of it. And it is certainly no way of working towards a better tomorrow or breaking the poverty cycle many children may find themselves born into.

Being motivated on the other hand will offer a child the inner drive to achieve their goals and to acquire the things that they need. It will help them to solve the problems that they will inevitably face throughout their lives. And it will support them with a wish to change old habits and inspire their efforts as they work towards new objectives, allowing them to set themselves more ambitious challenges or seize greater opportunities. Whether or not a child is developing the behavioural characteristics familiar to being self-motivated will depend on many things. But primarily it will be influenced by their experiences of setting their own goals, of identifying their personal expectations and of achieving them. Only then can they know how worthwhile the effort they are putting in is and what they are likely to achieve from it.

Offering the encouragement children need to achieve

As I said, children are born with tremendous self-motivation, repeatedly getting back up when they fall, trying again when their words are not understood and practicing basic skills hundreds of times to have reached the levels of perfection you can now see. As they get older these natural instincts can be damaged through the experience's and messages children receive. Whether this is through excessive expectations or limited opportunity, receiving little encouragement, too much or even from simply being praised for the wrong things. But if this can have such a monumental bearing on outcomes, how do we know what is right? How and when should you offer a child encouragement to act in a certain way and how exactly can praise be wrong?

When we use excessive praise or the promise of a reward, a child's natural instincts for self-motivation can be lost as they learn instead to be motivated through external influences, prompting the internal dialogue… "Do I have to do this?", "Does it count?," "Am I being noticed?" or "What am I going to get if I do?" Through this process, children are receiving the message that only the deeds with the rewards are worth doing, the bigger the reward, the more worthy the deed. And how you convey this message will teach your children a great deal about human interactions and relationships, the way the world works and how they should behave within it.

This "treat for tricks" technique used to be widely used by animal trainers. But even here, research has shown that from dolphins to dogs, a far better response is gained from signs of appreciation like a pat, hugs and smiles. And do we really want to utilise such outdated practices when raising our future generation of thinkers and problem solvers? Besides, a child is somewhat more sophisticated than your average puppy and their learning cannot be effectively supported through threats, bribes or rewards. Children need encouragement, feedback and disciplined environments if they are to achieve their full potential and it is in looking to accomplish this that will provide the encouragement and motivations a child needs far more than a sticker chart ever could.

Motivating children's ongoing interests

Whatever it is that you are supporting a child to learn, you can encourage their efforts through your approach provided you are mindful of the words and actions you choose and the implications of them. Children of all ages and in fact adults, continue to learn best when they are motivated by their own learning desires and when this is fuelled by a feeling of unconstrained exploration. While there are now more curricular goals for children to achieve than when they were a toddler, you can keep their motivation high by keeping these general principles in mind (Figure 8.1).

Figure 8.1: With some effective provocations and resources, children become motivated by their own desire to explore and learn.

- Look for elements of interest and further areas of exploration in the topics that have been given

- Help them to explore other topics as you find the links in their learning

- See how you can bring their learning to life with real examples or tangible materials

- Help them to apply what they have learnt as you take learning beyond the pages of a book

- And look to support their independence and interests, whatever they may be.

When you encourage a child you are expressing your confidence and trust in them and imparting the courage and belief they can have in themselves. This is why it feels so good to receive encouragement and praise. When genuine encouragement is offered, without judgement or underhanded coercion, this is a deeply nurturing and supportive process. From spontaneous delight and enthusiastic applause, to simply your presence, a smile or a hug, know that you are helping to foster a child's sense of pride and internal motivation. Provided that it is not used to control their behaviours or responses, heartfelt encouragement delivers concrete messages to suggest "I know you can do it", "You know the steps you need to do it" and "I'm here to help if you need me".

Offering nurturing comments

When you offer a child your comments, you need to be mindful of the power you hold to encourage ongoing belief in themselves or to effectively derail it. "That does not look quite right" will always invite a more encompassing response than "That is wrong". Realistic yet optimistic comments can be embraced and viewed simply as a part of the process of learning, rather than something to be feared or avoided as you help children to view themselves as a capable person, even when times get tough.

Encouraging children through your comments can then take a range of styles depending on the purpose. You can offer positive comments to help a child recognise and appreciate what they have achieved, to acknowledge that you have seen and applaud their efforts and persistence. Neutral comments offer basic instructions to help a child to organise and sequence their responses. Free from any emotional loading, these comments should inspire and encourage the next step or goal in their journey. And when constructive criticism is needed, be sure this is not taken as a put down, a personal attack or a nagging complaint.

When a comment is specific and directed at a child's actions, rather than the child, a compliment has the potential to highlight their success without seeking to cover up mistakes or failures. Similarly, constructive comments are also more easily received when they are directed at the task at hand, rather than the child. When used to draw focus to a mistake or problem that can be owned, a child can then use your comments to fix the problem and learn from it.

Understanding

Understand the impact your words and actions are having on children's self-motivation and the subtle changes of approach that make all the difference

Every experience a child is having with you is continuing to inform them about how future experiences are likely to feel. This is advising them of how they should behave and respond, even how they should think and feel. Through the expectations you place on them and the words of encouragement or guidance that you offer they are finding their place within this environment and developing their sense of belonging in it. Their need for a safe and secure environment is as strong as it has ever been, but the meaning of this is now changing. They are becoming more aware of how much control they have over their environment, of what they can do and the effect of their engagements with others. Because of this, their need for autonomy, challenge and self-direction is becoming more important and they will want to push themselves, their ideas and their capabilities further.

However, their realistic views of what they are capable of are still far from fully developed. They will become frustrated when a task does not come easily to them, when yesterday's best friend does not want to play with them or when the reality of the moment does not quite live up to their expectations. All of which can be exhausting in a body that still needs more nurturing and encouragement than perhaps a busy school day can find the time for. The result of which can be a frustrated bundle of misplaced energy, having lost the motivation for whatever assignment you consider important in this moment.

Embracing learning in a new environment

Through their early school years, children have a great deal to learn about what it means to learn, both in this environment, in this way and with this kind of knowledge. However, unlike future years of learning, they do not yet have the memories of past academic success to let them know they can do it. The continual challenges your children will be facing during this time are then being informed through every experience, with positive opportunities blossoming into later success. That said, do not be afraid of letting your children experience their mistakes. Children grow and learn from every decision they make, so let them make mistakes and learn from them. When challenges are faced with the right attitude and support, this experience simply adds to a resulting feeling of accomplishment. Through a series of activities and challenges that they can manage for themselves, children then learn to embrace their developing skills within a safe environment. It is then so important that children are given these chances to manage themselves, their environment and their goals (Figure 8.2).

Should you motivate children with the promise of a sticker?

Motivating children's actions and behaviours can often be associated with reward

Figure 8.2: Given opportunities to manage their own learning, decisions and mistakes children gain a positive idea of themselves as a capable learner.

techniques. Sticker charts or smiley faces that get moved along a rainbow from the bright sunshine to the raincloud and back again. But although these are done with the best intentions, we must look a little deeper to understand what is really occurring when we use these methods. Firstly, it is important to note that any practice you look to implement with consistency will become a familiar experience for your children. The messages they convey are constructively building and reinforcing your relationship with them, as well as their understanding and expectations of how the world and specifically your environment works. So, be mindful that you are not looking to instil motivation simply driven by the promise of reward.

The Sticker Chart for example simply focuses attention on what you want a child to do. But it does so by introducing the concept of "What are you going to give me if I do this?" When this is being used for something as deeply rooted as a child's intrinsic behaviours, you need to consider what it is doing to establish their self-worth, their self-motivation and an awareness of the consequences of their actions.

- Expecting good behaviour for a later reward is bribery

- Continual bargaining for behaviour leaves a child feeling controlled

- Children have a limited understanding of time, future incentives for desired behaviours now is setting them up to fail

- Behaviour charts that visually display misdemeanours or failure to impress are demoralising.

If you really want to motivate children to behave in certain ways, nothing can take the place of nurturing words of encouragement. And a better outcome would be achieved by introducing children to the satisfaction of a job well done and the consequences of their positive choices. Establishing a sense of their own self-worth will always be more powerful than any promised sticker.

And to achieve that, there are alternative approaches we can use

- Use timely consequences rather than bribes as you link children's actions to realistic and easily followed through outcomes, "If you tidy the equipment away we will have time for a story before lunch"

- Offer children a choice of correct actions they can take; "Which piece of work would you like to complete first?"

- Offer children an explanation as to why you want them to act in a certain way; "If you spill the water, we might slip. Help me with the towel so we can keep everyone safe"

- Children want you to be genuinely pleased with the efforts they are making, so acknowledge this by noticing their progress with descriptive praise rather than waiting for perfection

- We are all best at the behaviours we enjoy, so find the satisfaction your children can experience within the behaviours you want to see

- If you are trying to manage an ongoing problem, talk to the children about why this is proving difficult. You might like to encourage them to suggest a solution and talk about how this is working

- If you do want to reward, make it a surprise for a great accomplishment you have noticed, rather than a bargaining tool beforehand

- Focus on non-tangible rewards such as your time and encouragement, a smile or doing something fun

- And use rewards sparingly. As a one off they may help you to acknowledge and support a difficult time.

Motivating children through a belief in what they can achieve

You can help your children to develop positive beliefs about their capabilities through the empowering experiences you are offering them. And you can do this by letting them see the influence they have on their lives through their actions and the choices they make. When you offer activities that match their increasing capabilities and confidence levels, children learn to set and achieve their own goals. You might like to introduce a fun activity that you can share with your children within a time frame that mirrors their likely attention span. Growing salt crystals or planting a set of sunflowers are nice ways of doing this. You can then use these activities to role model your commitment to the task as you commit to its upkeep and support the children as they share in the experience.

Once you have found something that they want to do, share the experience with family members as you get others involved in the project and the processes involved. You can ask them if they have noticed any changes, focusing their attention on the activity and the learning that has come from it. Whose sunflower will grow taller? Which technique will have the better outcome? Does more salt result in a prettier salt crystal? Do the sunflowers need the sunniest place, or is being sheltered from the wind more important? With support, the children can then observe their personal impact on the project, learning how their actions are capable of influencing later outcomes. Along with inspiring motivation in a task they are interested in, you are also developing a strong foundation for more independent activities later on.

You can then add to this experience with comments like "Do you realise that we've been working together on this project every day for two weeks now?" You can point out how in the beginning you did not see anything happening, but because you did not give up and you kept at it, now there are lots of changes. Projects such as these that do not see instant results help children to appreciate that little changes can result in the realisation of big goals when they persist, working towards an end goal with commitment. Provided they do not give up, eventually they will achieve their goals.

This is also a lesson in delayed gratification, an executive function that supports their self-regulation, increased focus and the ability to become less distracted. By helping your children to see that efforts do not always result in immediate gains is a powerful personal attribute and life skill for them to develop. Made even more powerful here because they have discovered it for themselves, through personal experience. Over time, they will realise just how capable they are of influencing their outcomes and the world around them in both positive or negative ways. You can then remind them of this when they need a little extra courage and resilience when the inevitable setbacks challenge their resolve (Figure 8.3).

Support

Be supported in helping children to take more ownership of their goals, intentions and outcomes... even if they are not quite as you expected

We can all struggle with our motivation at times, finding it difficult to apply the effort and enthusiasm we need to complete a task. Whether this is something we have to do or a goal we had set for ourselves and were widely excited by in the beginning. We might respond in these moments by taking a break, planning a treat when the job is done or drafting in some additional help or guidance. Or maybe by giving up on the

Figure 8.3: "*Who can build a house for the three little pigs that can stand up to the puff of the wolf?*" (aka the hairdryer)! Offering a project that children can work on using the time, resources and groups they need ignites their passion for learning and a belief in what they can achieve.

idea and choosing something different. When it comes to a child's motivation for an assigned task, they do not always have these luxuries. They may have little choice in what they are doing or how they are doing it. Who they are doing it with or the level of support that is available to them. But that said, there are many ways that we can help them to find their motivation within assigned tasks and look to offer them the autonomy they need when we can.

Motivating children through their goals, intentions and outcomes

You can help your children to stay motivated by recognising their progress and achievements, even the small ones. You can do this by noting the individual tasks they have completed or the days they have worked towards something. As you help them to recognise their own achievements in this way, children can develop a strong sense of self and resilience. However, be mindful of the child who is working for the "well-done." These children are not as focused on the things that they can control as they should be and if you can support them to become motivated by intrinsic reinforcement, rather than the extrinsic rewards they are currently looking for, their natural motivation can continue in the absence of others.

Helping your children to choose, set and manage goals that are important to them is a fundamental life skill. As is the experience of having persisted to achieve these goals. The skills involved in identifying a problem and its source, understanding the steps that may be required to tackle it and feeling the power necessary to take action allows a child to develop skills fundamental to achieving success in life.

- Identifying a problem

- Understanding the steps to tackle it

- Being able to take those steps

- Feeling the joy of success.

Not only does this offer insight into what they want out of life, but also the confidence to go after it. It will also allow them to turn the inevitable challenges that they will meet along the way into positive situations that offer further growth potential. You will have heard of SMART targets, but what does this mean for your children? You can use these techniques to help children to focus their goals by considering the following stages.

Specific

Talk about a goal they would like to achieve, with as much detail as you can. Help them to set clear intentions, with a thought through focus. And guide them into thinking about whether this goal is something they would really love or just something that sounds interesting. The more excited they are by the goal, the more likely they are to achieve it.

Manageable

Help them to select a goal that requires several steps. While at the same time, make sure this is feasible with time and resources you have available or can acquire. Through the project, monitor their progress and be on hand for them to ask for any additional support or resources they may need.

Achievable

Help the children to be specific in identifying the outcomes they want to achieve. This may not be well known before they start, so use this opportunity to talk things through while energising their motivation for the project.

Realistic

Break the project down into manageable tasks and actionable steps.

Time

Estimate the time each step will take and schedule the times that children can work on the project. You might like to help them set a time frame for each step to be achieved by and support the children as they complete all of them, recognising and celebrating each step along the way.

Motivated to achieve the long-term goals

Sometimes your children's goals may take days, weeks or even years to complete, such as learning to read or write well. These long-term goals require great effort to stay on track, despite the pitfalls they may encounter along the way. In these instances it is important that we help children understand that it takes more than wishing to do something well to achieve it in reality. You can relate this to other long-term goals they may have and show them how working hard within a well-structured dream allows them to have a powerful impact on their world. This could be anything from wanting to be a footballer to travelling to Japan, owning their own horse or hosting the best birthday party (Figure 8.4).

You might like to create a vision board with your children as they develop a clear bigger picture of what they want to achieve. Help them think through what this dream looks like while thinking about the things they need to do to achieve it. If you then use this technique to plan for a long-term goal you will work towards together, their mood boards can provide a motivating, visual focus in a creative and fun way. In this way, as they visualise and progress through the steps, they are less likely to lose their focus when difficulties or lack of progress are experienced.

Struggling with a lack of motivation

If a child is struggling to motivate, this may be because they are expecting a negative experience. This may see them being unwilling to try or quick to give up when they do. If this is the case, you can start by giving them some easy wins or you might like to

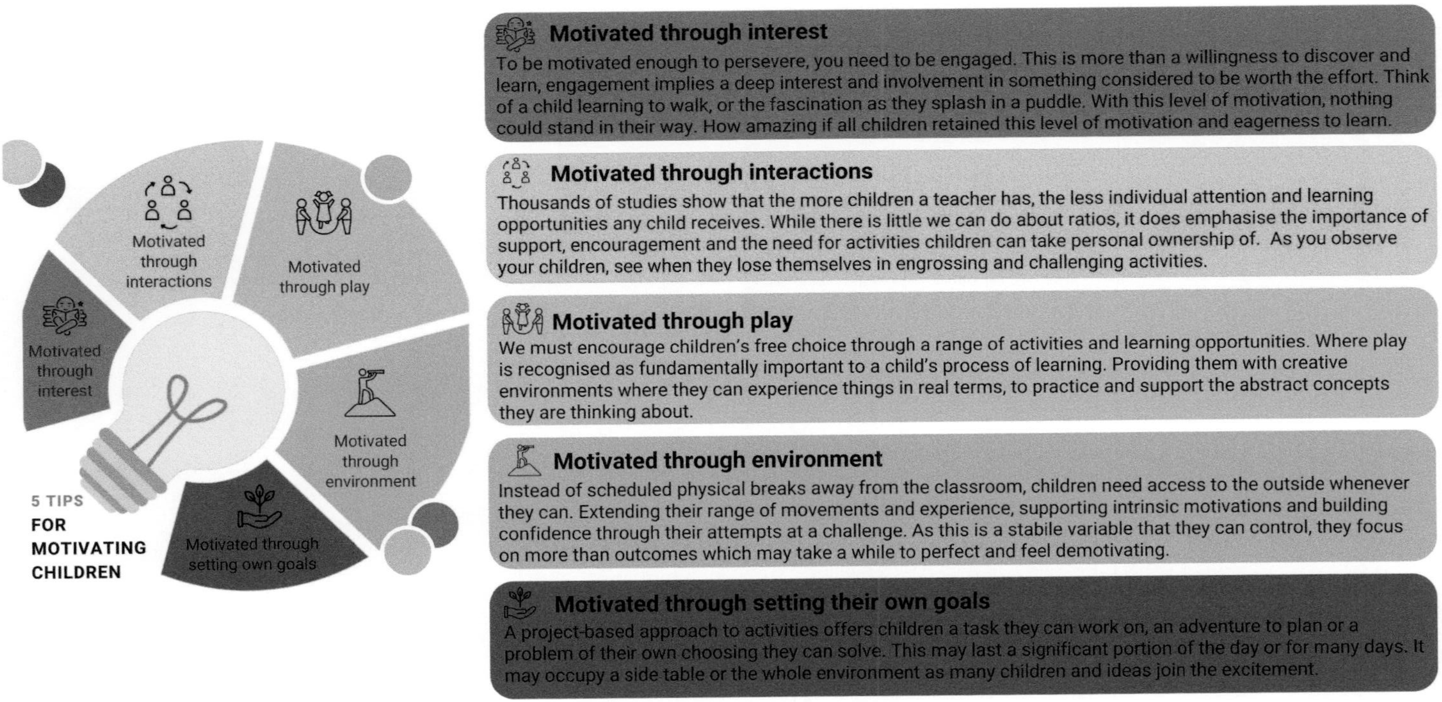
5 TIPS
FOR
MOTIVATING
CHILDREN
Motivated through interest
Motivated through interactions
Motivated through play
Motivated through environment
Motivated through setting own goals
Motivated through interest
To be motivated enough to persevere, you need to be engaged. This is more than a willingness to discover and learn, engagement implies a deep interest and involvement in something considered to be worth the effort. Think of a child learning to walk, or the fascination as they splash in a puddle. With this level of motivation, nothing could stand in their way. How amazing if all children retained this level of motivation and eagerness to learn.
Motivated through interactions
Thousands of studies show that the more children a teacher has, the less individual attention and learning opportunities any child receives. While there is little we can do about ratios, it does emphasise the importance of support, encouragement and the need for activities children can take personal ownership of. As you observe your children, see when they lose themselves in engrossing and challenging activities.
Motivated through play
We must encourage children's free choice through a range of activities and learning opportunities. Where play is recognised as fundamentally important to a child's process of learning. Providing them with creative environments where they can experience things in real terms, to practice and support the abstract concepts they are thinking about.
Motivated through environment
Instead of scheduled physical breaks away from the classroom, children need access to the outside whenever they can. Extending their range of movements and experience, supporting intrinsic motivations and building confidence through their attempts at a challenge. As this is a stabile variable that they can control, they focus on more than outcomes which may take a while to perfect and feel demotivating.
Motivated through setting their own goals
A project-based approach to activities offers children a task they can work on, an adventure to plan or a problem of their own choosing they can solve. This may last a significant portion of the day or for many days. It may occupy a side table or the whole environment as many children and ideas join the excitement.

Figure 8.4: 5 tips for motivating children in your school environments.

actively partner them with another child in a joint venture. As the children support each other in their efforts, they will also be modelling techniques and encouraging each other to see a project through to the end. And if the children are struggling to organise their efforts, the SMART goals can be useful for any task.

- Talk with them in clear language as you help them to clearly see what they need to achieve, only then can they see that they have achieved it

- Help them to remain focused on the outcome by managing any setbacks. Reframe their thinking and language as together you embrace these opportunities as teaching moments and take effective actions towards reaching their goal

- If this is where they typically give up, use the experience to understand the source of the difficulties as you work together to overcome them

- Turn negative situations into positive learning opportunities as you help their ideas, inspirations and goals to become a reality

- It can also be useful to focus their attention on lots of little wins within a different arena, such as crafts or physical activity as you help build their confidence in ways that they can take into all aspects of their life.

9 Supporting parents to nurture their school child at home

Almost as soon as a child starts school, they will become weighed down by the eagerly anticipated book-bag. Each evening, as a parent delves inside they will be greeted with the usual array of communications. And then, depending on the approach taken by the school and the age of the child, anything from daily reading expectations, a worksheet to practice letters or sums, a construction to depict the Eiffel Tower or a class mascot and diary that needs to somehow depict that they had a better time with this family than they did any other classmate!

When it comes to supporting a child with all the requests that come from the school, it can feel overwhelming. And the eagerness and capability with which it is embraced can mean different things to different families. How much space and access to resources they have for project work, the time they can dedicate to homework or the regular routines that allow for nightly reading practice can differ widely. As can the ease with which children respond to these activities and the experiences and knowledge of the adults that are supporting them. This may then raise a number of key questions. How is this impacting different children and different families? Does homework make a difference and if so, how much? Every night or is a big project better? Do we lose momentum if we miss a reading session? And how exactly do you get a reluctant child to stay motivated?

All of this can then be a struggle, children have been at school all day, they are exhausted and want to relax. Physically, as well as mentally as their young minds try to absorb everything that has gone on during the day. And as the adults supporting them, we can feel much the same way. However, one thing remains constant as research consistently shows the huge difference in attainment that can come from the experiences a child receives once they leave the school gates. In this chapter then we will take a look at what makes the difference, the things you should be concerned about and most importantly, where your efforts and attentions are best focused.

DOI: 10.4324/9781003327059-10

Knowledge

Know the importance of homework, while taking care not to overwhelm with the expectations that may be felt

In theory, homework offers a child the necessary time to practice their developing skills in ways that the school day does not have time for, whilst leaving time for teacher-dependent activities in the classroom. It offers children an opportunity to work independently, taking the time they need to absorb new information and practice as many times as they need without the schoolteacher moving on or a classmate interrupting. And as children absorb and incorporate this new information, they are developing a range of skills that are often more important than the task itself.

The way in which homework is approached and handled is then fundamental as a child learns about the process of independent learning and motivated discovery. By helping all the adults who are in a supportive role to understand this can then manage expectations and help them to see and buy in to its purpose. Along with feeling more able to offer the support that may be needed (Figure 9.1).

How much homework should be expected?

In the UK, children aged between four and seven years are in Key Stage One. During this phase of education, around an hour of homework a week is typical. This then raises to half an hour a night for Key Stage Two, for children aged seven to eleven years. In the

Figure 9.1: Offering a child a sense of autonomy in their learning, for example by choosing the book they take home to read, encourages the many hours of practice that proficiency needs.

US, ten-minutes a night is typical for children in Grade One, when they are aged between six and seven years; twenty-minutes for Grade Two when they are between seven and eight and thirty-minutes for Grade Three and so on is more typical. But each school sets their own expectations, so it is important that everyone understands what these are.

One of the most well-established findings in research on children's learning however, is that they cannot retain focus for long periods without breaks. About 20 minutes seems optimal to stop fatigue and allow the information to absorb, but this will vary with the age and character of each child. So, as the quantity increases as a child gets older, be sure to organise things in a way that allows for frequent breaks so that the learning can remain effective. If children are then struggling to achieve what they need to in the time frames suggested, consider what is at the root of the issue.

Adult support

Although it may be tempting to offer a child the help they ask for every time, research shows that the more a child receives direct support and supervision, the worse their learning and understanding of the material will be. So instead of setting expectations that require large amounts of help, ensure the tasks are manageable by the child. Make sure all the adults understand their role within the process and avoid establishing the learnt behaviour of immediately asking for help, possibly as an avoidance tactic. Once this happens, children are simply developing what is known as a "learned helplessness".

When a child is seen to struggle and become frustrated it can be tempting to jump in, but it is in these struggles that they are finding their way. And as they do succeed, a sense of accomplishment builds within them. Children should then be encouraged to put in the effort they need and praised when they do so, supporting them as they learn to work independently. The rule of thumb here is to have help available when a child needs it, but to minimise the amount of help that is actually provided.

If a child is floundering because they do not have the knowledge or ability to complete a task, they need help. No good comes from hours of struggling with something they do not understand. In this instance a technique known as scaffolding can be used. Whereby a child is provided with just enough support so that they can achieve the task. Then, gradually some of this support is removed until the child can begin to succeed independently. In this way the child understands that the help they ask for is about filling in the gaps to support their own knowledge, just like the scaffolding around a building. It is not there to hold them up or to be relied on to bear the load. Eventually you will be able to stand back completely, allowing the child to set their own goals and clear intentions, coming to you for support only when they need it.

What is homework for?

Homework gives children time and opportunity to practice the skills they are learning at their own pace. But it is also doing so much more than this. Learning of any meaningful kind is about more than discrete facts to be learnt, it is about concepts that need to be experienced and understood. Only then can they be used and adapted in other situations. These processes of learning that every child is engaged in are complex, interwoven and continual. As children revisit ideas and skills, they will adapt and perfect their understanding, while at the same time establishing dispositions for and attitudes toward the learning process.

When children are given work to do outside the classroom, especially when the tasks echo the topics they have been experiencing, they have these opportunities to revisit. Take for example an understanding of how weight works; how something can be heavier or lighter than something else and the meaning this might give us about what is inside. In school children can be told the knowledge they need. They can play with the concepts inside and out as they experience different weights. They might then feel how a jug of water weighs less as it empties, something they can feel throughout their whole body.

To then continue developing this deep and meaningful understanding of something, children need opportunities to experience them in a different context. They need to play with the ideas themselves, seeing how they relate to other experiences as they structure patterns within their learning. This may involve applying this developing idea of how weight works to a bucket of sand or a bag of feathers. Back in the classroom, when this is combined with the science and maths of transporting and pouring from different vessels, they are making connections in their learning. Developing a deeper awareness from having played with these principles. This will, in time allow them to know things without needing to experience it, skills that will inform visualisation and reflection, techniques they will rely on at every level.

When children are given opportunities to use and combine their newly acquired skills and abilities, they are learning how to perfect them. To arrive at answers that are meaningful to them and to understand what new abilities they need to explore next. But so much more than this, they are learning about their own abilities as a learner, something they will take with them into every new experience going forward. They are developing a frame of mind that is steeped in confidence, knowing they have the ability to think for themselves with the motivations and inclinations to do so. All of which is fuelled through the positive experiences of learning you can offer them. As you lay the foundations for the more complex ideas to come through tasks that are so much more important than simply repeating information (Figure 9.2).

Figure 9.2: Sharing the work they do at home with you in the classroom helps to make deep connections in their learning, understanding that knowledge is transferable, adaptable and multi-faceted.

Understanding

Understand how parents can encourage their child's learning without damaging their desire to do it

You've asked, you've told, you may have even threatened, but if you did not know better you would be sure that sometimes children are "choosing" not to partake in the behaviours you are asking of them just to be difficult. And when it comes to doing their homework, this is a prime example. Anyone who has tried to encourage a child to behave in a certain way when they have totally different ideas on the matter will know what a fool's errand this can be. If you have found yourself in the eternal loop of cajoling and bribing, you will have found that these methods just do not work.

The trouble with these approaches is that trying to "persuade" children to behave in a certain way will never end well because behaviour is a choice they will always make for themselves. Trying to coerce them into something will, at best, see them begrudgingly doing as they are told. And at worst, invite escalating issues and continual fallout, with lasting damage that will be felt by everyone. So, how do you support children to do the things they need to? How do you encourage your thinking, responding child to act in all the ways you would be delighted to see? Even when every day seems to bring mood swings as they get hungry, tired or are simply feeling under the weather?

Children are in the process of growing, developing and testing social boundaries. And they are learning from everything and everyone they see around them. As we have explored in previous chapters, any attempt at controlling them or getting them to "mind" simply because you say so may have serious repercussions down the road. Research suggests that one of the best ways to promote the behaviours you wish to see in a child is to offer an environment that models those desired behaviours. So, you need to create an environment where a child can observe, experience and learn how you want them to behave and they will develop the ability and in time, the habits to do so.

Engage children in wanting to learn

Firstly, if we want to encourage and promote highly successful educational outcomes in our children, we need to help them see the wonder of learning. Not as a means to an end or a task that needs completing, but through its opportunities to discover and learn things about the world and themselves. Children have no hesitancy in freely initiating or valuing the learning potential of play, so tasks set as homework can utilise this.

- When they play with real objects and materials, links will be made with what is familiar, making connections in their thinking and using greater levels of purposeful vocabulary

- Use fun experiences to teach key concepts, for example water, sand or mud play can be used to explore cause and effect, establishing relationships between actions and consequences

■ Experimentation, trial and error, inventiveness and risk taking where there is no wrong answer establishes resilience, persistence and curiosity within safe boundaries

■ Opportunities to reflect on their ideas, to think, consider, ponder and come back to as they need allows them to experiment with ideas before committing them as fact

■ All the while allowing misconceptions to become evident, allowing you to tactfully guide.

But while these activities are infinitely rewarding, they are also easily distracted from as soon as a screen is turned on. So, reserve the technology for when it is needed and instead offer them activities with open-ended, natural resources within spaces where they feel a sense of ownership. The natural explorations this may prompt might just see them encouraged into new areas of knowledge and challenge as they utilise their learning freely within their play.

Encouraging children's persistence

How do you encourage a child to continue with a task they are finding difficult when all they want to do is give up? When we watch a child learning to walk, they appear unfazed by the number of times they fall down as they perfect the skill. It seems to not occur to them to give up. And yet a few years later when that same child is learning to read and battling to decode the letters on the page, convincing them of the benefits of regular practice can seem a struggle.

Children have great energy and enthusiasm for the things they want to do. However, their frontal lobe, the part of the brain involved in delayed gratification, is not yet fully developed. This means they do not appreciate the benefits of working hard now for something that will not be rewarded for some time. Neither have they experienced how practising something, from letters to times tables, makes something easier and more enjoyable in the long run. It will take them many hours of work and disciplined practice to realise the level of competence they are perhaps capable of. While our awareness of delayed gratification is better, they have the energy and enthusiasm we lack. Our role is then to balance these two areas in our children.

But there are limits. The tennis player Andre Agassi would reportedly hit 2,500 tennis balls a day fired from a cannon; over a million balls a year as he perfected his craft. Undoubtedly, this had an enormous effect on his abilities, not to mention his muscle memory and reflexes. And he was fantastic, but he ended up hating it. In 1998, the UK government introduced Literacy Hour across all English primary schools. This intensive focus on reading was designed to significantly improve the abilities of children across the country. And although many showed improved performance, studies have shown that their love of reading significantly deteriorated. Just because they could, no longer meant they did. You do not need to look far to see stories of child prodigies and their amazing accomplishments after hours of practice. But what is less publicised are the stories of the children who gave up, the resulting mental anguish that comes from a lack of empowerment, their tendency not to thrive or do as well at school in other areas and the troubles that followed. Despite this, intensive periods of accelerated focus are still a commonly used tactic.

The root of empowerment is in having a sense of control, of being able to choose how to act and respond. But as a child is experiencing this, they also need to learn that their decisions come with consequences. To develop this sense of empowerment within a learning, developing child, we need to offer them experiences to try and to set their own goals and limits, even when this comes with mistakes.

Supporting children with their independent learning

When supporting children with their homework, we should not be focused on achieving flawless results. The learning that is coming from the experience is far more important than the painful pursuit of a perfect score. And when errors do happen, we can use this opportunity to talk over mistakes rather than being too quick to correct. Children need to experience making wrong turns within the tasks they are working on. As they experience that these too can be recovered from, they are developing an improved resilience that they will need when engaging in more complex learning down the road.

When children do come to you for help, use the opportunity to talk with them about what they are doing. Reflect on what has gone well, what do they know and what can they tell you? Then you can ask about where the struggle lies, encouraging them to put words to it. And as they do so, think about what might be standing in the way of them achieving their goals. If this is a lack of knowledge or a skill they do not yet have, they need help. If they seem worried or frustrated, help them to empty themselves of these emotions that may be standing in the way of free-flowing ideas, as you retain focus on what they want to achieve (Figure 9.3).

Figure 9.3: Projects completed at home are about showing children what they are capable of as much as practicing their skills and extending their learning.

When they are very young, their efforts won't be hampered by analysing the future or worrying about what happened in the past, living as they do in the moment. Whilst this does not always make for the best goal setting or decision making, it is where creativity resides. As they get a little older, some of this worry will creep in, so it is important that we help children to keep hold of their creativity and spontaneity as they develop a more mature outlook. And you can do this by giving them lots of opportunities to express it. After all, living in the moment is something we could all use a little more of from time to time.

Getting the family involved

Every child needs a degree of individual attention to achieve their best outcomes. They need activities that they are interested in, pitched at the correct level for their development and the time and support to grasp what they need before moving on. To do otherwise risks falling behind in ways that will mean they do not fully understand future lessons, leading to even greater deficits and a vicious cycle establishing that will affect their achievements as well as their belief in themselves as a learner and their motivation to apply the necessary effort.

However as I have mentioned, within busy classrooms, not all children can be actively engaged in the learning task and as such will not be receiving the attention or learning opportunities that could be leading to more positive outcomes. While there is probably little you can do to actively change class sizes, this does emphasise the importance of the support and encouragement a child receives from all the adults in their lives. Several studies show that when parents are shown recommended homework procedures, it is more likely to be completed on time. When they then share this and engage in them with their child each day, homework tends to be of a better quality and achieved with fewer arguments. Encourage all family members to talk with children about the homework they are doing, showing an interest and indicating its value in helping them to practice, to understand more widely and to have a chance to do things on their own.

When a family understands the benefits of home learning they are more likely to establish the routines and spaces that are required and to offer the support needed. But children also need to see the purpose and value of the exercise. The best way of doing this is in helping them to see how important their adults consider it to be, through the space, time and interest that it is given. This can be tough and there may be many other things that need doing, but the positive goals of it need to be kept firmly in mind, with any difficulties kept in context as you find its relevance and its pleasure. All the while being careful not to assign any negative connotations to the idea of home learning, reading practice and further discovery.

Support

Be supported in helping parents as they actively encourage their child's willingness to learn in the home

A developing child is beginning to explore their own identity, within this is their notion of themselves as a learner. They are learning that their opinions, their thoughts and their voice can all have meaning and consequences. With the level of their effort having an impact on their end goal. They are developing a belief in their own abilities and establishing a level of confidence to try something new. So, help them to see themselves as someone that learning and the efforts it takes is right for.

Meta research, that is the cumulative findings from many studies, show a correlation between the time a child spends on their homework and academic achievement. But only to a point. Whilst homework has its place, too much is counterproductive. Children need to rest and to give their brain time to assimilate all the information it has received during the day. To do otherwise results in "burn out", which will ultimately reduce a child's academic achievements and any desire to pursue them. If you feel that the demands being placed on children is too much, that their love of learning is being eroded or something is going wrong, raise these questions. Their ongoing desires to learn are more important than this week's schedule.

So, look to give children this ownership as they become responsible for what and how they are learning, at least moment to moment. With any activity, avoid being focused solely on getting it done or achieving its outcome and instead, think of the rich journey. Allowing children to see the results of their endeavours as you look to offer rewarding levels of engagement within carefully considered experiences. And when they do make a mistake, help them to see this as a step on their journey to better understanding and the self-motivation to stay with it. Knowing that as you do so, you are supporting the development of characteristics of lifelong learning, learning superpowers indeed (Figure 9.4).

Figure 9.4: There are not many references to escape slides in The Three Little Pigs, but the learning that happens when you give children this ownership of their outcomes is priceless.

Establishing a special place for learning

When looking at supporting children's learning in the home, the role of the adults is vital. Children are learning more from the attitudes and behaviours of those around them than they are anything else. And if these demonstrate a positive feeling towards the tasks the child needs to do, the whole experience is likely to be more positive in the long run. And this can start, if possible, by establishing a special place where they can learn, demonstrating how important this time is considered to be.

The Place

Getting the child involved, look to create a welcoming environment in which they can concentrate and learn effectively. Well-lit, quiet and away from distractions, this space should feel comfortable and have all they need, offering a consistent place to come to each day. Stock up on key resources together, complete with a storage box of all the equipment they might need. Not only does this avoid the nightly hunt for a pencil sharpener, but it also shows them the importance of the space and the meaning it has.

The Process

As children get older, they can get involved in making a plan about homework procedures, as the importance and value of it is explained to them. This might involve a consistent time and place, maybe calling it "study time" so that this time for deliberate learning can become routine. Even when no homework has been assigned. Others in the home could join them, sharing in a learning activity together, perhaps reading a book or learning a new skill.

The Time

For many children, insisting that this happens as soon as they walk in from school is too much. They are tired, they need food and a break. Settling down after dinner may work better once they have had an opportunity to unwind. Either way, the child should be involved in the decision. But avoid being too close to bedtime when they need to be relaxing, in mind and body for sleep.

The Experience

The most important thing you can do is to use this opportunity to nurture their curiosity and their motivation to know and understand. This is more important than the ability to perform any discrete skill, or to recite any fact. And know that their brain is growing and developing through every experience you are offering them, even the negative ones.

When you remove excessive pressures or a sense of failure from getting things wrong, children become more inclined to try. Thriving in an environment that promotes self-expression and recognises their own motivations and interests. While mistakes, risk and challenge are an inevitable and important part of their learning journey and must not be avoided, celebrate the efforts you see them making, even the little ones, as you create a safe, nurturing environment for them to learn in.

Getting down to it

So, you have your special place, all the equipment you need and the scheduled time is upon you. What now? Firstly, as we have been learning, learn best when they are motivated to do so. And this is best achieved when they have an interest in what they are learning, when there is a degree of independence and ownership of their efforts and when these efforts are aimed at their current level of understanding.

- Make sure it is pitched correctly

- Get them interested

- Get them motivated

■ Give them some independence

■ Give it some relevance.

Knowing that something is at a level achievable for a child's stage of development involves a level of understanding beyond knowing their age. It is embedded within the scope of their previous experiences and is displayed within their responses. No good comes from hours of struggling with something they do not understand or finding the work too easy, so being around to monitor is key. Offer help if it is needed, without directing their efforts or taking their ownership away and be aware of when "practice" becomes "boringly repetitive". If a child seems to be easily distracted or not paying attention it could be that the pace is too fast or too slow to hold their interest.

Think back to a time they spent all day engrossed in mastering a technique for something they were really interested in. The additional time they were spending at this task allowed new knowledge to develop and consolidate and this is what you are looking to do now. As their efforts are encouraged and rewarded, new ideas can incubate, fostering deeper understanding and a genuine love of the learning process. And supercharge this by having the adults around them becoming interested too.

Some children will be easily motivated and happy to put in the effort independently, either to please themselves or others or simply to achieve an objective. While the strongest motivations will always come from within, this is dependent on many variables and for some children may be quite a struggle. Once you have provoked their interest, help them to find their inner motivation by linking it to previous experiences where they have had success. Then look to notice and capture their independent efforts, even if these start small. When they do come across areas that feel more of a struggle, help them to see this as a natural part of the learning process. An opportunity for further learning, rather than evidence of them reaching their limits.

When it comes to completing homework, there may be set tasks that need to be given, but if you can offer children a degree of choice and ownership of what they are doing or how it is done, they can feel more part of the process. If you are looking to foster an independence in their learning, this cannot be second guessed or planned in advance. Instead, make sure they have opportunities and resources they can access independently and trust them with supported freedoms to pursue their motivations.

And finally, if they can see something real come of something they are learning or talking about, then the connections in their learning will be even greater enhanced as a personal relevance is added to the process. So, try to offer them authentic applications of what they are learning within realistic contexts that they can touch and manipulate, experimenting with ideas as they explore new concepts. When children can see a point to what they are doing, they will focus for longer periods of time. And if you can relate this to what they know and what they want to know, you can help develop truly GIFTED experiences of learning. And it is in achieving this that the next chapter will explore.

10 Supporting lifelong learning in the classroom

Throughout this book we have looked at the importance of nurturing a child's need to be happy, secure and supported by adults who know and understand them. We have looked at the holistic nature of their learning, their need to interact, engage, experiment and move. And all within environments that they feel a part of, where they are permitted to engage with resources and peers, share their ideas and work together as they challenge themselves, take risks and explore how far they can go. All of this is rooted in the quality and range of experiences and interactions a child is offered, in their home and throughout any teaching environment.

It is also widely acknowledged that through every sensory drenched, playful experience of their early childhood, children are learning at a rapid rate. Forming connections deep within their brain as they make the structures and pathways that later learning will depend upon. Then school starts and you can be forgiven for thinking that much of this has been forgotten. And yet multisensory, physical play and enquiry-based learning remain the most powerful methods we have for retaining memories and constructing knowledge throughout our lives.

When we think of children's education and classroom learning, it can become difficult to think beyond the curriculum we must follow or the learning goals a child is expected to achieve by a given age. But children's learning, especially within these foundational years is so much more diverse than any curriculum can capture. While you continue to support the ongoing development of their brain structure, you are also developing a child's attitudes towards learning. Through the opportunities and experiences you offer, you are establishing and reinforcing the neural connections essential to the learning process. But you are also developing their identity as a learner, as a thinking, capable individual, along with their expectations of all future learning.

In this chapter we will then look at the learning opportunities you are offering and how these nurture a GIFTED Learning approach. Whether you are familiar with

DOI: 10.4324/9781003327059-11

GIFTED Learning or this is something new, this chapter will help you reflect on how you engage children in the learning process through this lens. We will look beyond "what" is intended to be taught and the frameworks governing it, to consider how a child's learning is being facilitated. Mindful of how you help children become interested in knowing and understanding whilst helping them to recognise their own capabilities.

Knowledge

Know the impact of formal learning experiences and the tests we use to assess it on children's future dispositions towards learning

Your children are sharing so many experiences of learning with you. But what can be overlooked is how they are experiencing the learning process itself and what it means to try to learn. Every attempt a child makes is teaching them something more about the impact of their actions and whether the effort they are putting in is worth their while. And as you are no doubt aware from your own experiences as much as from your teaching, successfully mastering anything new has as much to do with effort and self-belief as it does with any level of intelligence or ability.

To support deep-rooted learning and commitment in the classroom, we do then need to know and understand the learning processes occurring so that we can engage our children within them. And the first thing to recognise is that children are not driven by the long-term goal of being great at something in years to come. Nor are they overly motivated by the prospect of passing another assessment. But give them opportunities to solve a problem they have a personal interest in or explore an idea that has just occurred to them and you can see what passionate, enthusiastic learning looks like.

How do children learn?

We have looked in previous chapters at how the brain "learns" through our experiences as neural activity is triggered through our senses. As you read (using sight or touch if using braille) or listen (using sound) to these words, physical structures deep within your brain are being stimulated. However, we tend to encode far less than we may think we would. As we have any experience, we bring the new things we are learning about into our short term memory, also known as our working memory, the part of the cognitive system where we process and apply reason. "Go to the third room on the right and get the blue book" are steps you will place in your working memory, ticking them off as you complete them. To add the numbers 23, 45 and 12 you start by putting those numbers in your working memory. How you go about the process of addition will call on deeper functioning.

Figure 10.1: Understanding what is being asked, listening to our friend, seeing what others are doing and making sure the lid goes back on our pen… all while practicing today's letters and getting them in the right place is a lot to ask of anyone!

The trouble is, our working memory has a very limited space, fading rapidly to be ready for the next sensory input. Hopefully there will be much on these pages that will stay with you as you read, but what about the person that walked past you when you were reading the last page? As we focus on some aspects of an experience more than others, the seemingly unimportant fades away within a few seconds as we filter out what we consider to be unnecessary and these details are virtually impossible to bring back afterwards (Figure 10.1).

There is then a limit to how much information a child can keep in their short-term memory before they need to allow their ideas to germinate. And they will focus on what is most relevant and meaningful to THEM in this moment, while other things fade into the background. If this is a desperate need for the bathroom or an upsetting comment that has been made, no phonics teaching programme is going to stand a chance.

To keep our memories, we then need to transfer information from our short-term into our long-term memory. With its essentially unlimited space, our long-term memory is where we keep the things that are worth remembering, with its content staying potentially for the rest of life. But this is a complex process involving a change in the pattern of connections linking the billions of neurons in the brain and interruptions and new demands can derail it, damaging the learning experience.

Researchers looking at memory development have shown children's abilities to hold things in their short-term memory increase dramatically during the primary years, doubling between the ages of four-years and six-years. However, a child's memory will not reach that of an adult's until they are around twelve years old and we must be mindful of the expectations we place on them. Following our instructions to "Get your book from your drawer, sit at your desk, and complete questions 1-3", at the same time as navigating a school classroom and its physical, social and emotional demands is then a tall order.

Children who are better at remembering will then spend more time doing the things that have been requested and as these tasks are naturally related to what a child is expected to learn, better progress will naturally follow. Enhancing memory can benefit children but so will making classrooms less reliant on it. Some researchers are actually suggesting that some diagnoses of ADHD are mis-diagnosed issues resulting from an undeveloped working memory. The last thing we want to be doing is then increasing the need of this one skill set in order to do well.

The limitations of tests for assessing children's progress

There are various styles of tests and assessments that you may have heard of or are becoming increasingly familiar with. An important tool for evaluating progress, both formative and summative assessment have a place in education. However, it is crucial that you recognise the limitations of the methods being used. For example, assessments that place emphasis on remembering facts are little more than a test of developing memory. You must also be mindful of the impact that taking assessments can have on a child and the limits of how well any one method can understand a child's learning. With outcomes that will vary considerably on the style of the test, the conditions of the day, even what a child had for breakfast.

Tests and assessments look to measure what a child knows, what they can do and what they can remember. However, they are not a very good method of understanding the knowledge a child has and they tend to be rubbish at seeing how good they are at applying that knowledge to anything real. But tests do have a strong direct and indirect impact on how a child thinks of themselves and how others view them.

Tests do have their place but like with any theory, remember where it came from, who wrote it and who and what it was intended for. In some countries, testing children's IQ is a common and influential practice, used to indicate potential outcomes and therefore determine many of a child's experiences through the education system. However, "intelligence" is a very wide concept and there is no way of measuring how smart you are. A person's IQ is now used as a legal definition for whether they can be expected to understand what is going on around them but taking its meaning too profoundly can be harmful.

Alfred Binet's original goal with his IQ test was to identify and remedy IQ deficiency. But they are not infallible estimators of intelligence or potential and whether the results are high or low they can do more damage than good. Using IQ tests to predict how well a child will perform in later years is also fundamentally flawed with most children performing significantly differently than their early test results may have predicted. And yet IQ predictions can be taken very seriously with products claiming to boost children's test performance a massive industry, with very little evidence to back up any such claims. Children do become better at these tests by practicing the skills they depend on, but this does not indicate any kind of rise in their knowledge or abilities. To develop their spatial awareness for example, they would be far better playing with blocks or physically exercising using their whole body than spotting the correct image on a page.

What happens when we test and assess children?

When we test a child, their success will depend on so many things including the language and techniques being used in the test, how the questions relate to their past experiences, even the attention being paid or the stress being felt at the time. And this is without the many external factors such as sleep, diet, things going on at home, as well as the distracting noises from outside. A test cannot take any account of the skills a child does possess if the testing structure does not reflect them. And yet their outcomes can go on to have huge impact, determining classes that children are placed in, the children they will interact with and therefore befriend, the opportunities and experiences they will receive, even the funding that will be directed towards them.

A time of learning should be a positive experience for all involved, it should have relevance, application and interest. And yet for many young children, regular assessment can introduce a source of undue pressure and stress. Inducing anxiety does not allow a child to perform at their best and can have long-lasting effects on their mental and emotional well-being, at a time when their attitudes towards learning are establishing.

A study by Stanford University gave a hard maths test to a group of people, mentioning in the instructions that "Studies show males out-performing females at maths", and unsurprisingly, they did. Significantly so, with the women expressing their increased anxiety. When the phrase "However that is not the high calibre of females such as yourself that have been handpicked for this research" was added, the stereotype was effectively removed. Research shows this belief in ability and how well you are going to perform is also strongly evident in children. Imply to a child that they are no good at maths by putting them in the bottom set and they probably won't be. Equally damaging is the notion of being very bright. As soon as challenges are met, a child will tend to give up rather than risk damaging their "bright" identity or assume the limits of their "brightness" have been reached.

As we have discussed throughout this series of books, every child you teach is unique, with their own pace of development and learning style. Formal assessments often fail to capture the nuanced progress that each child is making every day and when we focus our understanding of progress on test scores, we effectively overshadow all the small victories, personal growth and achievements that are occurring outside of its confines.

Formal assessments do not give any child the best opportunity to demonstrate what they can actually do and can also inadvertently perpetuate inequalities within the education system, significantly disadvantaging certain children. For example, not all children will be surrounded with the language and vocabulary being used, they won't have access to the same resources, experiences or support, affecting their performance as they get left further behind.

So, let me ask you a question. Why do we want children to know about the properties of a shape? Is it so that they are ready to name the number of sides and angles of a heptagon at a later date? Or is it so that they understand why an angle might be important or the different ways that shapes are used? If you want to know how well your children have understood something, you will get a better insight by giving them opportunities to discuss, experiment and think critically, rather than regurgitate expected answers. And far more informative than a score sheet, you can see the links they are making in their learning along with how well they are applying it. A more holistic and child-centric approach to assessment not only better serves the individual needs of each learner but also nurtures a love and appreciation for learning that extends far beyond the classroom or the test score achieved.

How can we nurture children's future dispositions towards learning?

So, how do we embrace a more balanced approach that speaks to the holistic learning of all children within a busy classroom setting then? Firstly, we can include observations, portfolios and project-based work to gain a more comprehensive view of a child's individual abilities and potential within naturalistic and stress-free environments. This will certainly move our focus from a "training children to deliver one-right-answer" approach and instead allow their developing curiosity, critical and reflective thinking, problem-solving techniques, even their social-emotional skills to be captured. And this certainly sounds like a more well-rounded education that would better prepare them for the challenges of the future. But we also need to remember how children learn (Figure 10.2).

Children need to experience their own success and to build secure confidence in their abilities as they develop the strength to meet and succeed within all the future situations they may face. You can promote this learning by offering appropriate challenges and risk and through the engaging resources you offer, along with sufficient time for children to get stuck in. If difficulties arise, let children see how they can resolve their own issues as they make choices and experience how perseverance and advanced thinking is rewarded. Allow children the time and space for free movement and quiet reflection as they revisit concepts and embed their developing expertise. Be on hand to promote their inquiries but avoid being too quick to intervene. And consider limiting activities that tend to dominate their attention with predetermined learning goals and instead capture their natural instincts to learn.

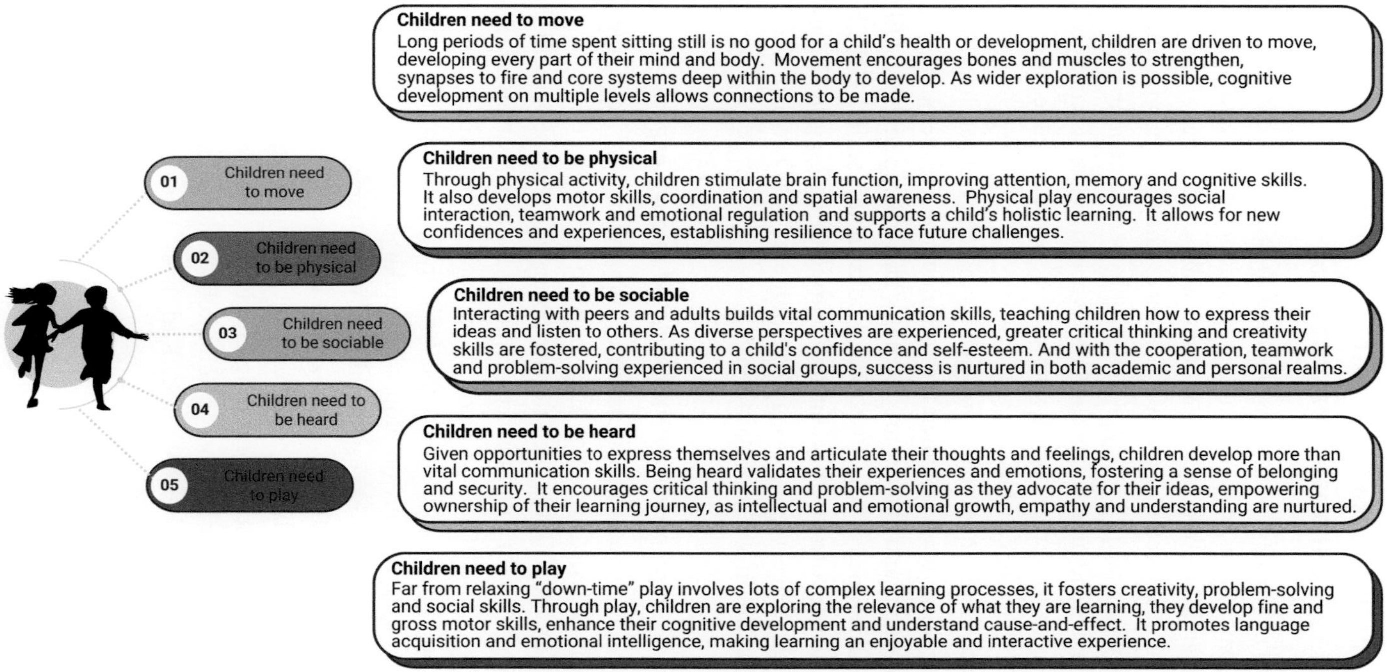

01 Children need to move

Children need to move
Long periods of time spent sitting still is no good for a child's health or development, children are driven to move, developing every part of their mind and body. Movement encourages bones and muscles to strengthen, synapses to fire and core systems deep within the body to develop. As wider exploration is possible, cognitive development on multiple levels allows connections to be made.

02 Children need to be physical

Children need to be physical
Through physical activity, children stimulate brain function, improving attention, memory and cognitive skills. It also develops motor skills, coordination and spatial awareness. Physical play encourages social interaction, teamwork and emotional regulation and supports a child's holistic learning. It allows for new confidences and experiences, establishing resilience to face future challenges.

03 Children need to be sociable

Children need to be sociable
Interacting with peers and adults builds vital communication skills, teaching children how to express their ideas and listen to others. As diverse perspectives are experienced, greater critical thinking and creativity skills are fostered, contributing to a child's confidence and self-esteem. And with the cooperation, teamwork and problem-solving experienced in social groups, success is nurtured in both academic and personal realms.

04 Children need to be heard

Children need to be heard
Given opportunities to express themselves and articulate their thoughts and feelings, children develop more than vital communication skills. Being heard validates their experiences and emotions, fostering a sense of belonging and security. It encourages critical thinking and problem-solving as they advocate for their ideas, empowering ownership of their learning journey, as intellectual and emotional growth, empathy and understanding are nurtured.

05 Children need to play

Children need to play
Far from relaxing "down-time" play involves lots of complex learning processes, it fosters creativity, problem-solving and social skills. Through play, children are exploring the relevance of what they are learning, they develop fine and gross motor skills, enhance their cognitive development and understand cause-and-effect. It promotes language acquisition and emotional intelligence, making learning an enjoyable and interactive experience.

Figure 10.2: There are many things we need to think about if we are going to nurture children in all the ways they need.

Understanding

Understand the importance of offering children GIFTED Learning and how this can enhance your teaching

Every day a child's view of the world is adapting in response to their own unique and highly personal experiences of it. When they speak, they are developing the courage to voice an opinion and the confidence that others will be interested in what they have to say. When they think and reflect on past experiences, they are applying their knowledge and learning they can adapt and approach problems in different ways as their self-motivation and independence flourishes. And when they are listened to, even if their ideas are different to the others being voiced, they learn to value their ideas and the depth of learning they are capable of.

As you facilitate these experiences, you give a child the respect that comes from your interest and recognition at a time when it is so influential in developing their identity as a confident, engaged and successful learner. This speaks of GIFTED Learning. Introduced and developed in the first three books in this series, GIFTED Learning looks at the Greater Involvement Facilitated Through Engaging in Dispositions and is the first stage of the Theory of Lifelong Development (ToLD) which we will continue to explore now we are in a school classroom.

GIFTED learning – Greater involvement facilitated through engaging in dispositions

GIFTED Learning recognises that if we want our children to learn, they need to be engaged in the processes of learning. They need to be able to think, to communicate and to adapt to new ideas. They need to have courage in themselves and their eventual capabilities if the efforts they will need to apply are to seem worthwhile and they need to be motivated to do so. They need to be able to imagine things they cannot see, to reflect on past experiences and to have the curiosity to want to find out. Dispositions towards these responses can only develop when children have the time, permissions and resources that allow them to experience them. When their attempts, even when not perfect, are recognised, facilitated and valued. Because if these natural inclinations towards learning are not facilitated, children begin to disengage when they could have had every opportunity for their world to ignite (Figure 10.3).

We have a tremendous impact on our children's lifelong learning and development trajectories through every experience we afford them. But we are not the first to have had this influence, these trajectories have been establishing through every experience they have received so far. The children you see every day were born eager to learn and understand their world, hard-wired to utilise and develop these dispositions and natural methods of learning in any way they could. Every time they have been given opportunities to do things for themselves, they have experienced the benefits of independence and self-motivation. As they have had new ideas along with opportunities to try them

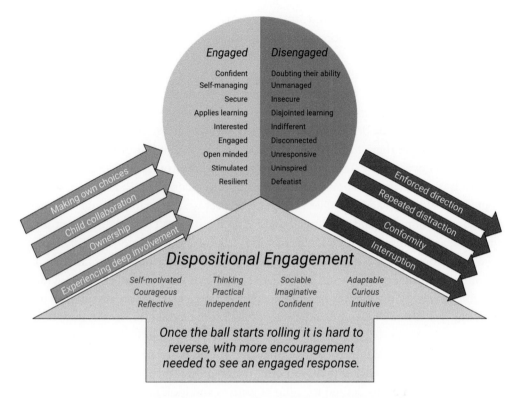

GIFTED Learning
Greater Involvement Facilitated Through Engaging in Dispositions

Figure 10.3: GIFTED Learning – Greater Involvement Facilitated Through Engaging in Dispositions. This is the first stage of the Theory of Lifelong Development (ToLD) and asks you to consider what happens to learning when you take the potential for engagement away.

out, they have seen the purpose of their imagination and intuition. And when given opportunities to make their own choices, testing their boundaries and taking risks, their courage and resulting confidence has been given opportunities to blossom.

However, traditional classroom experiences of learning can replace many of the freedoms children have had to experience these dispositions as their environments, tasks and social groupings become more controlled. Unable to pursue an idea for as long as they need, to be autonomous in the decisions they are trialling or unable to access the resources or environments that will allow them to explore an idea fully, many children find these limitations difficult and confusing. After all, it is their natural instinct to want to engage in these ways and the conformity and governance of formal learning can cause them to disengage from the very processes they are there to receive. GIFTED Learning brings our focus back to the child in front of us, in all their multi-layered complexity, now and throughout a lifetime of learning.

Developing the dispositions of successful learners

As we have discussed throughout this book, children are complex little creatures who are continuously learning and developing in holistic and deeply individual ways. Affected by their environment, the people in it, the autonomy they are given to engage and every experience that has gone before. Trying to neatly split these complex processes into "learning areas" and "lesson objectives" will affect each child in very different ways, with varying degrees of success that has little to do with a child's intrinsic potential. However, this is what happens when the learning outcomes drive the experiences we offer through our teaching. But what would happen if we reversed this expression? What if we stopped allowing ourselves to be driven solely by external agendas and started instead to focus on the children we are there to teach? I know, a crazy idea… but just give me a minute.

We are all governed by curriculums and statutory frameworks, department guidelines and levels to be attained. There is little we can do to change this, but there is nothing stopping us adding an additional lens to see the impact we are having through our methods, our environments and our interactions. And the impact I am talking about is that which we are having on our children. I am not talking about additional testing, no one needs any more of that, but instead tuning into the most powerful way our children have of communicating anything to us… through learning to see and read their behaviours.

Being driven by the child is not a new concept, in fact, if you do any project-based work you will already be embracing these ideas to some extent. However, how do you determine the progress being made or the value of its outcomes? Do you begin with the child and the behaviours they are embracing? Or do you start with the list of objectives you are hoping to tick off? As you offer children these rich activities, do you avoid becoming focused on its desired learning objectives and look instead at the journey the child is on? Think for a moment about what really engages you in something, motivating you to make real strides forward. Whether this is learning a new skill or playing a sport you enjoy, reading a favourite author through to the end or becoming lost in a film enough so that you finish it. Do you think that your source of enjoyment is likely to be exactly the same as everyone who had enjoyed the same thing?

A child's emotional engagement is a deeply important part of the process and experiences of learning that a child does not see an immediate need for can seem futile and unworthy of any great effort. Looking to systematically download knowledge into the minds of developing children is then never going to be a rewarding learning experience. This will impact any potential achievement, both by them losing interest in the process and also through its effect on their self-confidence and motivation across other areas. You may have seen this reflected in a child's attention skills, concentration and persistence, with behaviours that may read as disruptive or be misunderstood as a lack of ability.

If we then add to that the pressures to conform or to respond in ways they may not be developmentally ready for and high levels of stress can be experienced. And as these become linked in the child's mind, the whole process of learning can become associated with negativity. A link that will become more firmly established with each experience, until an expectation or fear of failure may see a child look to avoid the styles of learning they have been experienced within.

If instead we allow children to get stuck into the learning process with increased levels of agency as they explore tricky concepts, we can promote and extend their knowledge and understanding. If we allow children to collaborate with the resources and permissions that allow them to react to evolving interests and unexpected events, they can use these experiences to make deep connections within their learning. And through authentic experiences, with relevance and purpose we can continue to engage children in their deep-rooted dispositions towards learning.

Support

Be supported in establishing GIFTED Learning throughout your teaching environments

Children's methods of learning and understanding their world do not change simply because they are in a school classroom. To make the deep-rooted connections they need within their learning, they still need to touch and manipulate the world around them, they need opportunities to experiment with resources and concepts, freely manipulating and combining new ideas. They need time to intellectually process, question, practice and explore as they make deep-rooted connections in their learning. And if you can provide your children with creative environments, tangible experiences and a little autonomy, their intrinsic motivations, curiosity and independence will bloom.

But to do all of this we need methods and techniques that will allow us to focus on unique and individual children within a busy classroom. And whilst being mindful of external agendas and demands, avoid becoming overly driven by them. Only then can we embrace this foundational period of development, nurturing the developing minds and capabilities of the children sat in front of us today. Ready to receive the memories and experiences that tomorrow's learning will rely on.

Make learning GIFTED, fun and manageable

Children are active and independent thinkers who learn best when allowed to combine different processes in response to their deepening understanding. To simultaneously cater to the learning needs of all your children does then require well planned environments inside and out. Preferably with free and instantaneous movement between them as independent thought is facilitated and gratified.

When you permit your children this spontaneous exploration of a range of well-considered activities, their learning, imagination and creativity can be actively promoted. They can try out various ideas, initiating and manipulating their understanding as they investigate and make decisions, persisting in ways needed to make sense of their world. So, as you think about the opportunities your children have access to, think about how free they are to repeat and manipulate as they need, consider how GIFTED your focus is, how much Fun they are having and whether it is Manageable throughout the day.

GIFTED

Regardless of the activity or the learning goals you may need to achieve, try to keep the development of their foundational, lifelong learning skills in mind. These are so important that we will discuss them in turn through the final chapters of this book.

Fun

We all work harder at the things we enjoy doing, especially when we can see the relevance of doing it. So, make learning fun and purposeful. Learning to read will take a long time with much to learn and practice, but the excitement and benefits of it can be shared straight away.

Manageable

Don't let the work become overwhelming. If children are beginning to fidget during a whole class activity instead of focusing their attention on you, it is because their bodies are telling them they need something different. Don't fight it, use it. Take learning outside, embrace their natural learning instincts and create lasting memories that can be steeped in the knowledge you want them to learn.

A large part of the learning process is assimilating new knowledge; considering it, questioning how it fits with what they thought they knew and making the necessary adjustments. This can't happen effectively if more new knowledge is continuously being presented to them. Children need time to play with concepts, to see them represented in books, to explore how it works in various environments and to talk about what they are thinking about. Their academic work is important, yes, but so too is socialising and discussing, playing and moving, trialling and experimenting. When a child is seeking to master something complex, they will provide their own motivation to succeed, provided you can ignite their interest and curiosity. Once practiced at this, children will find it easier to persevere through increasingly complex tasks with ease.

- Consider your environment and the opportunities you offer by looking at the dispositions your children are engaging in

- Talk with children about any areas receiving limited attention and consider activities to address this

- Offer lots of diverse, practical and authentic experiences of what you are teaching

- Let children see something real come of something they are learning about as you enhance their connections and add personal relevance to the process

- Children need to feel positive about the efforts they make, so let them see the impact of their efforts

- Offer time and opportunities for children to self-direct their learning, revisiting areas as needed

- Recognise the value of time and space to ponder and wallow as children explore their ideas, consider concepts and see what they can do

- Let children work within different social groupings

- Be on hand to supply the support and information children request, rather than all the answers

- Offer meaningful, measured and focused praise arising from the effort children are putting in

- Give every child opportunities to find their voice, to reflect on what they have done and achieved

- But remember, this may be easier in small groups than in front of a whole class

- And don't forget, sensory learning is still as powerful now as it was when they were babies!

And lastly, remember that the learning process should never become uncomfortable. If they are squirming and fidgety, they need to move. If they are distracted and don't seem to be paying attention, they have probably overfilled their short-term memory already. And never use their learning as a "punishment." If you want to kill a love of maths in a child, make them do it as something that must be endured before the good stuff can start. If you want to destroy their love of reading, keep them in to practice while all the others go out and play. Forcing children to learn is simply making children disengage from learning and damaging their intrinsic motivation. Remember, a child wants to learn, if they are suggesting otherwise, something is getting in their way (Figure 10.4).

Figure 10.4: Children need to experience their learning hands on, within environments that can accommodated a GIFTED learning approach.

Section 2

Introduction

The Nurturing Childhoods Pedagogical Framework in the Classroom

Throughout this book, we have explored how learning is a complex process. That it is holistic, continuous and deeply rooted in the moment and affected by the knowledge and understanding of every adult gatekeeper governing it. To that end, this book and the others in the series have been written to support you as you reflect on your knowledge and understanding of all the holistic facets of a child's learning process. And as we now turn our attentions to applying these principles in practice through Section Two, I would firstly like to introduce you to the Nurturing Childhoods Pedagogical Framework (NCPF) and the ABCs of Developing Engagement (ABCoDE) (Figure S2.1).

As a pedagogy, the NCPF runs alongside any statutory curriculum or framework you are working with, offering an additional lens through which to understand the actions and behaviours of any learner. It supports you as you consider the opportunities you give your children and how these are engaging them in their learning. It does this in ways that are both universal and timeless, independent of any changes in your curriculum, new statutory initiatives or even the country you are regulated by.

The nurturing childhoods pedagogical framework and the ABCs of developing engagement (ABCoDE)

We know that a child's experiences of learning are deeply affected by the environments and opportunities they have available. Their responses are influenced through the relationships they have established, the interactions being facilitated, even the distractions outside the window and what happened at lunchtime. Along with every previous experience they have ever had. This means that every teaching moment you share with a child and any outcomes you are looking to achieve will be as diverse as the children in front of you. Trying to write a framework focused on predetermined goals and

DOI: 10.4324/9781003327059-12

KEY FEATURES OF THE
Nurturing Childhoods Framework

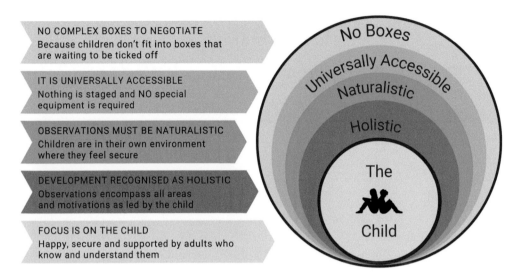

NO COMPLEX BOXES TO NEGOTIATE
Because children don't fit into boxes that
are waiting to be ticked off

IT IS UNIVERSALLY ACCESSIBLE
Nothing is staged and NO special
equipment is required

OBSERVATIONS MUST BE NATURALISTIC
Children are in their own environment
where they feel secure

DEVELOPMENT RECOGNISED AS HOLISTIC
Observations encompass all areas
and motivations as led by the child

FOCUS IS ON THE CHILD
Happy, secure and supported by adults who
know and understand them

No Boxes
Universally Accessible
Naturalistic
Holistic
The
Child

Figure S2.1: The Nurturing Childhoods Framework: Unique for its central focus on the developing child and the behaviours they demonstrate rather than any learning goals that serve only to draw focus away.

objectives and expecting our thinking, impressionable, mobile and highly vocal children to simply follow is then the source of many classroom frustrations. When we would be better placed looking to understand and embrace the natural characteristics of inquisitive children, their conscious and unconscious need to know and understand and offering learning experiences that fully engage them.

To offer children the experiences and provocations they need to engage in highly motivated learning, while ensuring the sense of agency, involvement and connection that every learner needs, we must then embrace their uniqueness, rather than expecting our children to conform. Luckily our children are very good at demonstrating how well we are doing, reflecting our success through their behaviours and responses. Provided this is where our attention is focused, we can understand a great deal about their learning and development. And this guided awareness will then allow us to facilitate the deep-rooted dispositions underpinning a child's learning journey as we become more aware of our impact on it.

In Chapter 10 we spoke about the concept of GIFTED learning and how we can facilitate our children's greater involvement in the learning process when we understand and enable their engagement in the dispositions that are fundamental to it. This spoke of curiosity and motivation, of being reflective, intuitive and capable of diverse methods of thinking. The NCPF will now allow you to embrace this concept throughout your teaching practices (Figure S2.2).

Whether you are familiar with this framework or it is your first experience of it, the first thing to notice about the NCPF is that it is child centric. Positioning children and their responses in the moment at the centre of our observations, it looks to support our understanding of engagement, noticing the child's behaviours and reactions and recognising what this is telling us about their learning and developing dispositions. Rather than focusing on expected learning goals and assigned targets that can see us meticulously following a lesson plan that may be missing its mark.

To do this, the ABCs of Developing Engagement (ABCoDE) directs our attention firstly to the child or children in front of us as we ACKNOWLEDGE all that they are. It then asks us to look at the BEHAVIOURS we are facilitating, how we encourage children to respond through our actions and the opportunities we give our children to think for themselves, to make choices and participate. And it does this whilst remaining aware of what a child's behaviours are telling you as the CHARACTERISTICS or dispositions underpinning them are developing and allowing these learning processes to take root.

As it looks to recognise learning as a complex process, dependent on THIS child, in THIS moment, in THIS environment it embraces the holistic, infinitely connected and continually evolving thinking and learning that is occurring. And it allows us to respond to the multitude of variables that inform and determine their success. Because of this, the NCPF does not require any specific environments, specialist equipment or staged activities that will be received differently by every child. There are no narrowly defined expectations, targets, lesson plans or agendas and you certainly won't be looking to fit children into any boxes. But to do this, we need some tools that allow us to look quickly, to look without blinkers and to really see. To this end I would firstly like to introduce you to the OPTED Scale, which you can think of simply as "what are your children opting to do?"

Introducing the OPTED scale

The Observed Preference Towards Engaging in a Disposition Scale (adapted from the FOLLEP Scale, (Peckham, 2021)) was devised to support my own research into children's engagements. Heavily influenced by Farre Laevers and his work with well-being and engagement scales, the OPTED Scale allows us to observe the full range of developing characteristics as illustrated in the blue petals of the Framework Flower. Whilst remaining mindful of the different environments, pedagogies and provocations that influence this process. It also allows us to reflect on a child's behaviours over time in a holistic and continual way as they demonstrate their tendencies to engage – or

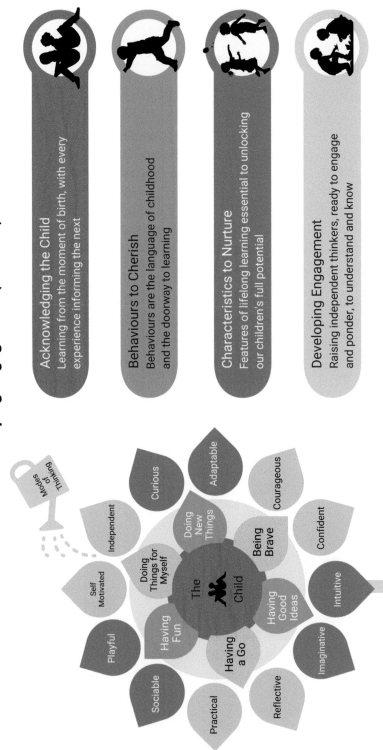

The Framework Flower and the ABCs of Developing Engagement (ABCoDE)

Acknowledging the Child
Learning from the moment of birth, with every experience informing the next

Behaviours to Cherish
Behaviours are the language of childhood and the doorway to learning

Characteristics to Nurture
Features of lifelong learning essential to unlocking our children's full potential

Developing Engagement
Raising independent thinkers, ready to engage and ponder, to understand and know

Figure S2.2: The Framework Flower and the ABCs of Developing Engagement (ABCoDE): Sitting alongside the Nurturing Childhoods Pedagogical Framework and acting as an additional lens through which to view it, the ABCs of Developing Engagement (ABCoDE) helps us to look at children's deep-rooted developments firstly through ACKNOWLEDGING the child and all that they are, then through observing their BEHAVIOURS or what is often termed the language of childhood, whilst remaining mindful of the developing CHARACTERISTICS that are un-derpinning them

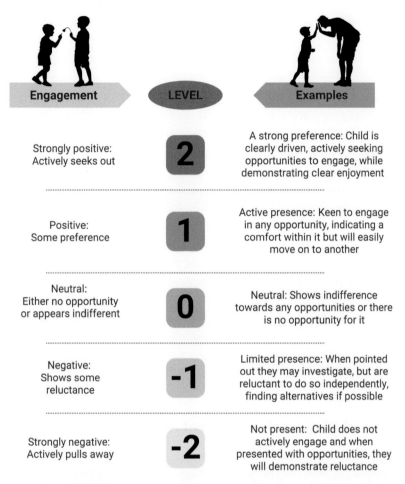

Figure S2.3: The OPTED Scale - Observed Preference Towards Engaging in a Disposition: The OPTED Scale allows you to understand what you are seeing at a deeper level and offers ways of tracking the impact of your decisions on all of these processes.

retreat – from certain characteristics, indicating their developing tendencies towards them (Figure S2.3).

The OPTED Scale is a five-point scale that allows you to quickly and easily gauge a child's involvement in any of the NCPF characteristics. A rating of zero sits at the middle, indicating that there is no opportunity or inclination towards this characteristic in this moment. Moving upwards, an observation can record a +1 for some indication or a +2 if the child is showing a clear indication of being engaged in this way. Moving downwards, an observation will record -1 if a child demonstrates some reluctance towards this characteristic or -2 if, in this moment, they actively pull away, showing a clear disinclination.

The first thing to note about the OPTED Scale is that it is used to record an OBSERVATION, not a CHILD. So, while during an observation on a Wednesday morning in April you may record self-motivation with a -2, there could be many factors affecting this. However, when you repeat this observation you find you are frequently recording self-motivation at -2, this may tell you something about how this child's disposition towards being self-motivated is developing. It might also tell you something about the opportunities you are offering to children to do things for themselves. Equally it could tell you a lot about the activities scheduled on a Wednesday morning or the staff on rota. So, let me repeat, this scale is used to illustrate a child's preference as they engage in a range of dispositions in this moment, it is not a label we affix to the child.

Because of its versatility it can then be used to monitor developing trends towards engagement, the development of certain dispositions within a cohort, even offer reflections on a given environment, set of activities, teaching styles or the adult behaviours that enable them. With every experience we have informing our next, these trends are then of great importance. If a child is reluctant to show self-motivation this Wednesday morning, they will use this memory to inform their next response when given an opportunity to be motivated. If this was a one-off, this will have little impact. However, if this is a trend you are seeing developing, for any number of reasons, negative trajectories could be establishing and we must then look at these scales through a range of variables as we gain a greater understanding of the influences on children's learning experiences.

The theory of lifelong development – In childhood (ToLD-C)

As our children have been progressing through all their environments of learning, they have been gathering years' worth of experiences. These are now informing their behaviours and the development of their dispositions, with trajectories becoming more pronounced. This can be a positive process as children become more confident, self-motivated and imaginative learners. Or these can become negative, as self-conscious, reluctant and closed off character traits develop, influenced by any negative or limiting experiences the child may have found themselves in. To demonstrate this effect more clearly, we can look at the Theory of Lifelong Development - in Childhood (ToLD-C) (Peckham, 2021) which suggests that children do not learn in a bubble, but as a social being, responding to all the stimuli around them and influenced by everything that has been experienced before.

ToLD-C postulates that lifelong development is a direct consequence of our experiences, rooted in those we establish in our early childhood. It suggests that key experiences as unique as each individual, facilitate the extent and nature of our dispositions towards different responses. When permitted and endorsed, our positive experiences promote our effective engagement, allowing for secure dispositional development which we enjoy through the characteristics and abilities that we are realising. This then allows for more positive outcomes which in turn feed into our next experience as this cycle shown in yellow, begun in early childhood, continues throughout life influencing our areas of personal development and ultimate future outcomes.

Unfortunately, not every experience is a positive one and the cycle can be negatively influenced just as easily as negative or absent experiences impact a child's opportunities or inclinations to engage, shown in red. Their developing attributes and realised outcomes are affected, placing the cycle on a negative tilt. As their future experiences and engagements are negatively informed, the cycle continues and this effect is further enhanced (Figure S2.4).

As children respond within their social and physical environment, they are interpreting everything around them, using their previous experiences of something similar as a reference point. Adding to this are the dual motivations of their internally driven behaviours and any real or perceived external expectations, continuously influencing, motivating and driving their next response, whether this is positively or negatively. This includes real and perceived success and failure, opportunities and limitations, permissions and boundaries.

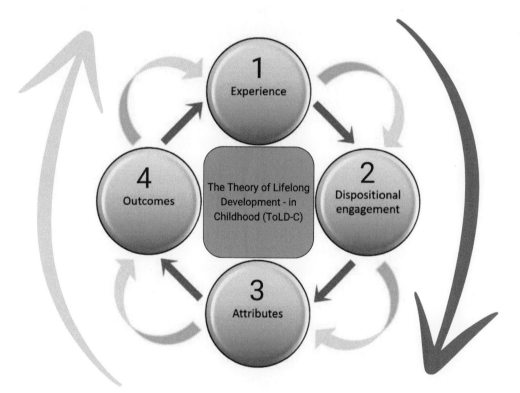

Figure S2.4: The Theory of Lifelong Development - in Childhood (ToLD-C):
Children are continuously gathering experiences and learning so much through each one. These experiences are informing their behaviours and their dispositions towards a response. This can be positive as children become more engaged learners or negative, influenced by limiting experiences they may have found themselves in.

This says a great deal about our responsibility in determining these trajectories, demonstrating the importance of the opportunities and experiences we offer as well as how we respond to children's engagements with their learning and the potential effect on their future dispositional development. As I mention throughout this book, every experience of learning is also teaching a child so much about what it means to try to learn. When these experiences are fixed, non-negotiable and subject to the high stakes of not succeeding first time, we must question the influence this is having on our children as unstimulating experiences today simply demotivate the learner, increasing the likelihood of disengagement tomorrow.

This cyclic portrayal of continuity and progression within lifelong learning and its potential for a negative tilt is recognised by many in the field who are concerned for the negative impacts our children are demonstrating in their motivation, curiosity, engagement and the learning skills being enabled. When external criteria, such as the demand for discrete, measurable skills become the focus of a child's experiences of learning, the resulting long-term effects on their ToLD-C cycle can be dramatic. With negative aspects of the cycle remaining evident, even when more positive opportunities are then introduced. As declining ease within thinking and decision-making processes have been noted, along with children's responses to opportunity, collaboration and risk, relationship skills and their sense of belonging and well-being all being impacted. As more formal classroom-based practices are employed as children progress through subsequent years, at the expense of dispositionally engaged learning, the negative impacts on the cycle are increasingly at risk and a framework to both recognise current influence and support positive engagement is then required.

Techniques are then needed to understand the impact of these experiences and the developmental trajectories establishing. To that end I will now introduce you to MICE and TOADS as we look at this effect and demonstrate the impact of a range of variables on a child's engaged experiences. And as you begin to look at children through these lenses, you will learn more than whether the contents of any programme or curriculum have been delivered and instead see children mastering their naturally evolving dispositions. You will observe not only deep-felt learning, but also what it means for your children to try to learn as they become absorbed in every experience you share as a step on the monumental journey that they are on.

But more than all of this, it is my hope that you will reflect on teaching as more than influencing this terms academic results and realise the lifelong magnitude of the experiences you are offering. And the responsibility we have to raise this recognition in the hearts and minds of all the other adults in their lives. Whether you are teaching one child or responsible for the development of hundreds of minds.

Potential implications on practice – MICE and TOADS

Whilst some children enjoy traditional teaching methods, learning well and making good progress, others struggle to engage when making the transition to more formal learning environments. With effects felt by children and teachers alike, the resulting behaviours, especially low-level disruption, has been cited as the main source of stress for most teachers across a range of countries. More exciting teaching methods may then be sought along with universally implemented programmes or wholesale purchase of expensive resources. I would suggest that long-term improvements to child engagement is better served through an informed understanding of what learning means and how it happens, along with recognition of the children you are working with and the experiences they need as has been echoed throughout this series of books.

So, I have introduced you to the concept of GIFTED Learning, and how important it is that we recognise children's dispositional development if they are to effectively engage in any learning experience. We have seen that a child's experience of learning in the moment are unique to them and heavily influenced by the environment, interactions and opportunities around them. As well as by every previous experience that has led to this moment. I have spoken about the potential you have every day to facilitate a child's dispositions through the experiences you offer, that when these experiences are well matched to a child's needs, this is reflected in their dispositional engagement, informing the attributes that are developing and influencing the outcomes your children will go on to achieve. I have even introduced you to the OPTED Scale to help you observe dispositional engagement in the moment. But how do you know whether a child's ToLD-C cycle is on a positive or negative tilt? How do you know whether the experiences or environments you are offering are well matched? And how would you begin to select the areas or practices to work on that could have the most influential change?

The education profession is rooted in the notion that children's developmental potential is enriched through the experiences being offered, rather than a predetermined biological or inherited trait. This implies great opportunities, but also great responsibility, relying heavily as it does on the permissions of those aware of and advocating for its motives. From the discussions, involvement, grouping and choice being permitted to the distractions, location and encouragements being offered, children's experiences are heavily influenced and governed by the actions of the adults around them. As are their resulting levels of engagement. When we begin to acknowledge this impact and recognise that a child's experiences and responses do not occur within a vacuum, we can begin looking at the variables that are limiting or enabling dispositional engagement, including access to environments, resources and time, location and social interactions, as well as additional expectations, activities and agendas.

When children are given a voice, choice and social opportunities, when their need for multimodal learning is acknowledged and when culturally responsive pedagogy embraces their natural propensities for learning, a child's sustained engagement will visibly increase. Experiences required to nurture this dispositional engagement are found in children's autonomy and are afforded through their choice of location and activity. It is nurtured when they have a shared ownership of the learning experience, rather than expected conformity, especially when participation is permitted at a personal level. As well as opportunities to corroborate and discuss ideas with peers, with sufficient time and resources to make these experiences authentic. Once engaged, children demonstrate more confident and secure learning as they actively apply new knowledge with openminded interest. Self-managing, children appear stimulated by the process of learning and resilient when additional effort is required.

However, forced interruptions, repeatedly being distracted away from an area of interest, enforcing direction within a given activity and long periods of expected conformity will all see children disengage as these practices effectively lose sight of a child's intrinsic desires to learn. Becoming insecure and unable to effectively manage their responses, children often appear disconnected from their learning, doubting their abilities as diverse accomplishments are often overlooked and application can become fragmented. Growing indifferent to the experiences being offered, children often appear unresponsive, uninspired and quick to lose interest when met with any challenge. And once child engagement wanes, previously effective conditions that may have seemed to promote engagement can fail to see it reintroduced. With deep concern for the long-term effects of these changes, I have then developed the Method of Improved Childhood Engagement (MICE) and TOADs as we acknowledge the impact of Theory, the Outcomes experienced, the developing Attributes and resulting Dispositional engagement.

Introducing MICE and TOADs

We have spoken about the potential for a child to have both positive and negative influences affecting their developmental trajectories. If you want to nurture a child's learning and future engagement, you need to be mindful of these influences with an informed understanding of the child's ToLD-C cycle and the tilt that it is on. And we do this by looking at the cycle in reverse through a process we can remember with the acronym TOAD. Conducted at the beginning and the end of the process, TOAD is completed by a trained practitioner with a good knowledge of the child, their interests as well as the content of the school curriculum, its schedules and any additional key information. And at the end of the process, it can be utilised as a measure of improvement as barriers to engagement are evaluated and addressed (Figure S2.5).

We have seen the multi-faceted learning that occurs within children and the need to recognise children as individuals, TOAD then offers a way to see beyond the homogeneous group that can be typical within school systems to consider what best suits individual learning needs. It allows you to observe beyond academic requirements or specific goals as your familiarity of a child's dispositional tendencies is gained through their displayed behaviours, with deep level development that can then be demonstrated to leadership and governing bodies. Whilst this is not to be considered deterministic or prescriptive, this process offers an indication of children's tendencies within their learning cycle, the impact of previous influences and an indication of dispositions that may have previously been neglected or avoided, all the while focusing attention on the natural links as it offers a baseline understanding of a child's ToLD-C cycle.

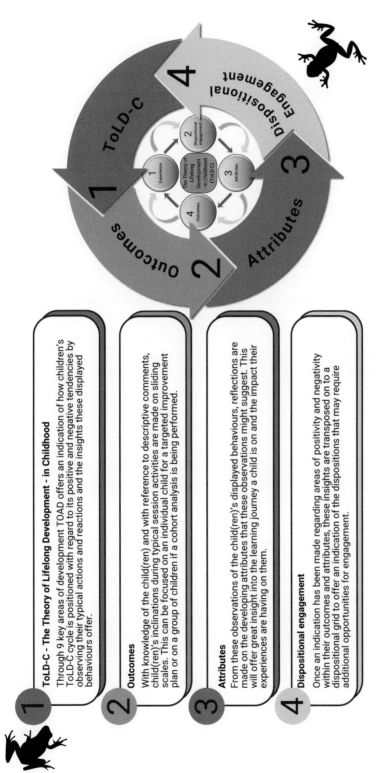

ToLD-C - The Theory of Lifelong Development - in Childhood

Through 9 key areas of development ToAD offers an indication of how children's ToLD-C cycle is positioned with regard to its positive and negative tendencies by observing their typical actions and reactions and the insights these displayed behaviours offer.

Outcomes

With knowledge of the child(ren) and with reference to descriptive comments, child(ren)'s inclinations during typical session activities are made on sliding scales. This can be focused on an individual child for a targeted improvement plan or on a group of children if a cohort analysis is being performed.

Attributes

From these observations of the child(ren)'s displayed behaviours, reflections are made on the developing attributes that these observations might suggest. This will offer great insight into the learning journey a child is on and the impact their experiences are having on them.

Dispositional engagement

Once an indication has been made regarding areas of positivity and negativity within their outcomes and attributes, these insights are transposed on to a dispositional grid to offer an indication of the dispositions that may require additional opportunities for engagement.

Figure S2.5: TOAD allows you to recognise the effects that past experiences have had on a child's ToLD-C Cycle. By learning to see what their behaviours are telling you, you can understand how their dispositional tendencies are developing.

Underpinned by the insights of TOAD, the Method of Improved Childhood Engagement (MICE) then turns its attention to the experiences you are offering to your children. It helps to identify potential barriers to their engagement and enable dispositional opportunities. It does this by firstly considering your environment and its resources and then with focused reflection on the external influences placed on children and the personal choices and freedoms this permits. Full training and materials are available through the Nurturing Childhoods Academy, but for now, let us take a look at the principles behind the processes.

Firstly MICE takes you through a 10-Step Programme that you can use to evaluate your teaching styles, environments and practices through a dispositional lens. It supports you to conduct a dispositional audit of the environment and your resources, children's access to these and to address any barriers. It then looks at the external influences on a child's learning experiences, including teaching delivery such as class teaching, group activities and supported learning. Distractions such as those introduced through time constraints and interruptions are also captured, along with the locations being offered and whether these allow children to make connections in their learning and the encouragements children are being offered. It then looks at the intrinsic influences being demonstrated as children respond within these environments. It does this by looking at the discussions that are entered into, the level of involvement that is being demonstrated, the groupings such as pair, group or individual work time that is being permitted and the element of choice that children are experiencing.

Observations are then employed to capture child engagement throughout their learning dispositions, noting how they are impacted by the environment, the levels of autonomy that are permitted and the interactions that are taking place. As you capture coded pedagogical styles and corresponding dispositional engagements using the OPTED Scale, along with rich descriptions of events, these form a focal point for further discussion. If repeated during a period of targeted improvements, they can be used to observe the impact of evolving practice or periodically to offer comparison. MICE can be used to capture practice across a range of sessions as different approaches are trialled, across different environments or to gain a deeper understanding of cohort development. For example, if engagement of summer born children is a concern, potential disengagement during numeracy sessions or specific aspects of an individual's engagement are of interest, focused comparisons can be conducted in these areas. Providing tangible evidence to support discussion, target setting and improvement, TOAD informs and underpins the tailored application of the 10- Steps of MICE, which may collectively form part of a schools ongoing evaluative processes, its practice development portfolio as well as offering a valuable addition to key performance data (Figure S2.6).

The NCPF in practice

At Nurturing Childhoods we talk of nurturing the full potential of every child, but this requires the opportunities and permissions to find what this means for themselves as we

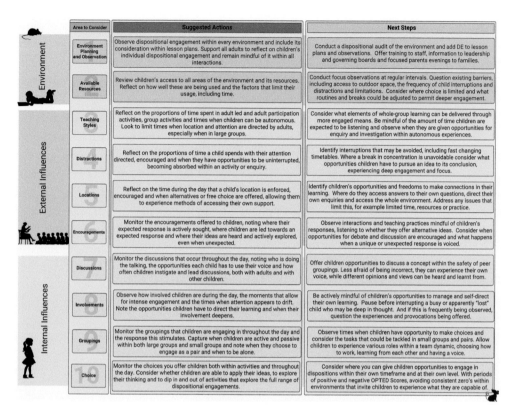

Figure S2.6: The Method of Improved Childhood Engagement (MICE).

recognise and capture the greatness of every child, not simply the narrow set of criteria we are looking for. Through wider definitions of achievement we can capture the full potential of children's dispositions and provide them with the skills, knowledge and motivation to achieve in a society of tomorrow that we can't even begin to imagine. Where their creativity and ingenuity is both stimulated and driven, where they are excited to continue learning and capable of problem-solving in a variety of contexts, displaying innovation, analysis and enterprise, able to cooperate and manage setbacks with resilience. Our school curriculums must then ready our children for the present and a future, that for us all is largely unknown.

So, when you engage with a child, be aware of how you are impacting the development of these dispositions through the permissions you extend and the messages you convey. Through diverse practical and authentic experiences, encourage discussion as they trial and approach new ideas, letting them see and feel the impact of their learning as their ideas take shape. Allow children to be independent as they self-direct and explore their own direction of enquiry, reflecting on what they have done, using their intuition and revisiting as they need. Consider the world of possibilities you can explore as you value the unusual or unexpected teaching moments. Be sure to see any lack of knowledge, yours as well as theirs, as areas to be explored. And take the time to genuinely engage, showing them you are interested in what they think, that you trust in their efforts and believe them to be meaningful and worth pursuing.

Chapters 11–16 will explore each of the six observable behaviours detailed in the NCPF and the dispositions underpinning them. Chapter 17 finishes with a look at the modes of thinking that unite them all. We will look at their importance, how we can develop a child's abilities and desires to explore them and the practices, environments and experiences that facilitate them now. As we do so you will notice a distinct lack of key stages, class years or grades as this framework applies to all learners, regardless of age. And whilst your attention needs to adapt in line with the child in front of you, the framework and its ability to support and nurture our children's learning remains constant.

Nurturing school children to do things for themselves

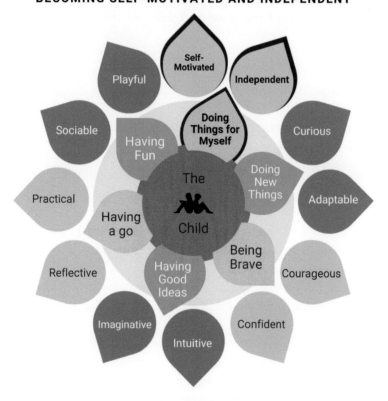

Figure 11.1: Doing things for myself - Becoming self-motivated and independent:
When we nurture a child's opportunities to do things for themselves, they develop the self-motivation and sense of independence that allows them to do it for themselves next time.

DOI: 10.4324/9781003327059-13

In this chapter we are going to focus our attentions on nurturing children as they do things for themselves, developing the self-motivation and the sense of independence that allows them to do so (Figure 11.1).

When children are given the chance to do things for themselves they can experience the power of their own abilities. And through these opportunities, to see what they can achieve for themselves as they learn to see themselves as a successful learner. As they realise the benefits of becoming more self-reliant, they gain positive experiences of their own achievements, learning what it means to persist with a task and to be motivated in something they have an interest in pursuing.

From this comes a self-motivation that sees them push through difficulties and try again, establishing a work ethic that will remain with them as their challenges become more complex. This then results in a wide range of positive outcomes and the recognition that may follow. But this takes self-belief, courage and opportunity if children are to develop this way of thinking. They need to experience an element of autonomy within the teaching methods used, as an element of trust and accountability is placed within them. When this happens, children learn that they can voice their own thoughts, to stand apart from the crowd and to be recognised for their own unique abilities and potential.

Knowledge

Know why it is important for children to do things for themselves

When children are offered opportunities to do things for themselves, they can experience the benefits of being self-motivated within a task. When given a degree of autonomy, they can recognise the benefit of persistence if they are to be successful and the inner strength that this sometimes requires. Within this approach, they may experience setbacks or difficulties, but rather than becoming frightened or demotivated by them, they learn the enjoyment and reward of a challenge, learning to embrace struggles and initial setbacks as part of the learning process. Finding a personal motivation to succeed, even when others may be faster, find things easier or when immediate rewards may be lacking.

Once this is established, children experience what it means to be driven by their own, more meaningful goals without fear of unfavourable outcomes getting in the way. They see the intrinsic rewards of their efforts as they recognise these abilities within themselves, experiencing the joy of reaching their goals. And through this independence, children are learning self-reliance; that they are responsible for their own decisions and actions as they avoid becoming dependent on others for the things they want and need.

They are discovering a strength in themselves as they understand that oftentimes, success and failure are very personal things. They are learning to have a voice and what it means to take responsibility, to own their choices, realising that their actions can and do influence their outcomes. And when this begins from an early age, children become used to this sense of independence in their learning and its outcomes. Happy to work hard, with courage even if they feel unsure or not yet understanding. And with the bravery to stand alone as they become an independent thinker, with a confidence in their own abilities. Furthermore, when children are no longer dependent on external gratification they are no longer limited by expectation or the need to conform in established ways. In later years this allows their motivation to continue even when their degree of success may deviate from what is expected.

Understanding

Understand how to develop a child's ability and desire to do things for themselves in the school classroom

When we can develop a child's independence, they are no longer reliant on the assistance of others as they learn to take personal responsibility for their actions. And in doing so, their true potential and personal growth can be realised, fuelled by the experience of independent success. But to do this, children need to experience a level of autonomy. They need to be permitted freedoms within their actions and decisions as they learn what it means to try (Figure 11.2).

To develop these tendencies, we need then to establish a self-motivation within children. Rooted within their belief in their ability, it is essential if they are to achieve their long-term goals, whether this is understanding weather cycles or reading with ease. Promoted through positive experiences of continuing in the absence of your direction, validation or continual support they no longer fear the absence of these things.

Figure 11.2: From their first experiences of the school environment, children need independent access to resources and their environments allowing them to explore an idea, to test a theory and practice what they know.

Something which can easily see children unsettled and distracted. With space and time for open-thinking and without the pressures and boundaries that are often experienced, children learn to persist despite a challenge or setback as they recognise a resilience within themselves.

When offered a range of opportunities that they recognise as productive or of value, children have a greater willingness to apply the effort and practice they need to succeed. Strengthened every time an obstacle is faced and overcome, they begin to focus on their own, potentially bigger goals, fuelled through experiences of personal success. Driven and directed by the child, these experiences offer greater ownership of their achievements and the outcomes being realised. All of which is essential when encouragement, external praise or immediate recognition may be lacking.

When given opportunities for a wider range of experiences, unpressured and with a degree of freedom within their actions, children can become driven by personal desires, which is naturally an independent process. Through experiences of retaining this free choice, a tendency to always "play it safe" or to simply follow expected choices is avoided as courageous leaps of faith are attempted. And safe in the knowledge that if the situation becomes too much, it can be amended, children learn to grasp opportunities before they are taken away.

When experiences are not overly structured by others, actions and opinions can become self-driven as children independently discover their own ambitions and skill sets. And when we can help develop this sense of their own abilities, children develop the drive, resilience and determination to succeed as a personal commitment to tasks establishes that sees them persist for as long as they need to realise their success.

Support

Be supported in offering practice, environments and experiences where this can be explored

When you can, offer children opportunities to select their own activities, free from expectations or their forced participation. When you can give them the time, space and freedoms to identify and work towards their own goals they will move at a pace that is suited to them. And in an area of interest that matches their individual abilities and needs, they are much more likely to feel motivated to persist.

Whilst children will need your support and guidance, too much support can encourage dependency and is often better coming from a peer group. So where you can, allow children to choose who they work with and the group sizes that form. Children will also need to develop an understanding of the time and effort various tasks may take. This may involve some initial flitting, but when you can combine this with some mindful offers of support as it is needed, the self-motivating satisfaction of experiencing their own successful outcomes will allow for a deeply rooted sense of achievement to develop. Provided their attentions are not forcibly drawn elsewhere.

To encourage children to do things for themselves they need activities where they can become valued for their independent thoughts, ideas and opinions. As they find their voice within a group dynamic, their personal reputation in the group

Figure 11.3: Group tasks that invite independent thoughts, collaboration and negotiation result in experiences of learning that children are far more motivated to persist with.

becomes defined. As children are recognised for the strengths they bring, a positive sense of themselves develops (Figure 11.3).

As you allow children to experience both their successful attempts and their frustrations, these simply become a part of the learning process. And when they next experience difficulties, they will be less inclined to use avoidance strategies or be quick to give up. If you can also offer personal experience of the benefits of persisting by focusing on the efforts they are applying and the small wins they may be overlooking, you can show them the importance of their motivation.

As children experience managing their own time and taking necessary risks they learn to push their abilities and become accountable for themselves as they get to know their strengths and weaknesses. As you stand back and observe the bigger picture, you can appreciate the progress that is being made as you guide them along their learning journey. If you can do this without becoming solely focused on learning goals, you can embrace the unique possibilities this might offer and help children to do the same.

Within environments where accomplishments are recognised and encouraged across multiple areas, their individual efforts can be recognised and acknowledged. So, try to limit how much you constrain a child's efforts through predetermined agendas or the limitations of a prescribed outcome. And instead offer periods of uninterrupted exploration rooted in their own enquiries as you promote their self-motivated tendencies.

These opportunities to be self-reliant allows children to experience the benefits of persisting through long periods of effort with unguaranteed results or immediate gratification. And are reinforced through enjoyment within a task, through an element of competition, whether internal or external and through the motivating realisation of what they can accomplish.

12 Nurturing school children to do new things

Doing New Things
BECOMING CURIOUS AND ADAPTABLE

Figure 12.1: Doing New Things - Becoming Curious and Adaptable: When we nurture a child's opportunities to do new things, they can experience what it means to be curious and adapt to changing circumstances, allowing these dispositions to develop.

DOI: 10.4324/9781003327059-14

In this chapter we are going to focus our attentions on nurturing children as they do new things, or do things in new ways, developing the curiosity to want to and the ability to adapt when things change (Figure 12.1).

As children embrace the learning opportunities they are offered every day, we want them to do so with curiosity and interest. We want them to be inquisitive, noticing the new information presented to them as they challenge their own abilities. Keen to understand and question the new information they are receiving as they think deeper about the things they know. However, when children do something new for the first time, they may sense a lack of familiarity or direction. They may feel unsure how to respond or the things they need to do next. To be in a position to learn from these new experiences, children cannot then be afraid of these feelings. And this is rooted in the positive experiences that have come before.

Children need to feel comfortable and secure enough within their surroundings to be able to adapt to the changing demands and approaches they may be presented with. Then, when ready, they can seize the opportunities that come their way. Trying different approaches when new experiences present a challenge as they persevere through difficulties, rather than being too quick to give up. Embracing new learning, happy to try different solutions and motivated by the experiences that have come before.

Knowledge

Know why it is important for school children to do new things

When you offer children different experiences you are introducing them to the joy of learning something new. You are widening their world view with every new experience as they become interested in knowing where things come from and understanding why. As they experience what it means to search for answers and experiment, combining information and intuition you can ignite their passion to learn. Developing a deep interest within them that is more rewarding than simple direction.

As they learn to question "What if…?" you can introduce them to deeper methods of thinking as they learn to debate, to become analytical or sceptical of surface knowledge. Embedding within them a need to understand, to challenge, to investigate and to see what comes next. Motivated by the curious mind you are nurturing as they learn to investigate what they are told, unafraid of mistakes (Figure 12.2).

Through these experiences, children are learning what it means to feel confident in not knowing as they continue through these stages of learning something new with confidence. They develop an ease during times where there may be a lack of direction, capable of moving their understanding into areas unknown. And they are developing an open mindset as they allow their understanding to develop, remaining flexible and reactive to the process without being thrown by it.

Children who have a wide range of positive experiences develop methods of adapting, happy and confident to try something new. They can focus on their achievements with the ability to change direction when something is not working. Reacting to changing circumstances and wider considerations as they experience the growth that is possible through change. Through the diverse opportunities that are offered to them, children can see a wide range of personal strengths emerge. And with each opportunity they are given to try, to experience and respond they are developing an enhanced view of their own potential.

Understanding

Understand how to develop a child's ability and desire to do new things in the school classroom

Figure 12.2: From a young age children have a great desire to understand, using this curiosity to challenge what they think they know and to ask the big questions. Like what would happen if I added more water to the mud… and how cross is she likely to get if I try?

When you offer a variety of areas for exploration, curiosity can develop across a breadth of interests, with the enhanced benefits this makes available. But if we want to develop a child's ability and desire to do new things, we need to ignite this curiosity within them. This will naturally come from the positive experiences they have had before of being able to question and explore the different options that are available to them. To ask the questions others might not as they learn to explore further, seeking clarification and validation, challenging what they think they know as they discover the thrill of knowing more.

Through enriching activities you can offer children a breadth and depth of understanding that would not be offered otherwise, perhaps exploring uncharted territory. When you offer wide ranging projects for children to become involved in they can experience flexibility in their thinking and approaches. Provided they are encouraged to take their own lead as they discover what interests them, rather than being guided purely by expectations. As the implications of any decisions they are making can be considered and alternative pathways trialled, validated and tested. As well as questioning their own performance through the new experiences being offered.

Being able to adapt to unexpected experiences also allows children to embrace different solutions and the opportunities that change can bring. When they can become resilient to unforeseen circumstances, the challenges and difficulties they face in their learning can be smoothly moved on from as setbacks are proactively managed with flexibility. You might like to restructure the day from time to time as they learn to adapt to the changes you introduce, rather than being unsettled by them. Invite them to alter their response within a task when things work differently than expected or when someone else has a different idea.

However, to remain confident during these times of diversity requires a sense of security. You can support this adaptive approach by introducing a range of opportunities gradually, incorporating distinct experiences that utilise different skill sets. Encouraging and enticing children into different areas as they explore at their own pace. When you can then introduce children to more than one linear way forward within a secure, nurturing environment children realise this is nothing to fear and begin to experience the benefits of adaptive thinking. They are then more likely to embrace new opportunities, rather than finding themselves limited by a fear of change.

Support

Be supported in offering practice, environments and experiences where this can be explored

To develop the curiosity needed to try something new, children need opportunities to become involved. To actively seek answers and to listen and respond with interest to the questions being raised. But to think at a deeper level children need to experience applying their inquisitive tendencies as they explore their understanding, learning to unpack concepts rather than simply accepting them. And all of this is just a little easier with a friend at their side.

As you allow children to try a wide range of experiences and available resources you can develop their confidence within the full range of their abilities. As they develop their skills within open-ended and evolving situations, they can experience what it means to revise their approaches and adapt their original plans as their degree of comfort grows. It is only when children are denied these opportunities for deeper understanding that they feel the deep frustrations that you might be all too familiar with.

You need then to allow children to experience the potential of their curious, active mind. Allow them to explore an enriching environment with exciting prospects that encourage them into uncharted territory, with the time and friends around them that foster this deeper curiosity of the world. You can support their investigations if their direction becomes a little lost but avoid giving them a predetermined outcome every time. Instead, allow them to respond to their needs in an environment that is adapted to them and to move on when they are ready.

Ignite their love of discovery by offering exciting new experiences, introduced with a promise of intrigue and interest. When combined with opportunities to freely explore, children learn to not simply accept ideas at face value. Where materials can be investigated and experimented with, children explore with a healthy scepticism as they draw their own conclusions. Developing a curious interest in what things

Figure 12.3: Experimenting with different ideas, trialling different methods and changing the approach is how children have learnt so much in such a short time. Don't lose these natural lifelong methods of learning just because children are getting older.

mean and where insight might come from as they find things out for themselves. Supporting this joy of discovery you can then motivate their achievements beyond a "that will do" approach (Figure 12.3).

Use new opportunities to trial different group dynamics. As they engage with others they can become aware and respectful of different ideas, adapting their own responses as they learn to incorporate a wider understanding. In doing so, children learn to think on their feet as the enriched and evolving "collective view" allows for additional strengths to emerge.

Being comfortable when adapting to different situations requires positive experiences of being flexible. However, this is a process that is achieved when change is not overtly and frequently exerted on children, so handle with care as you offer flexible and adaptive experiences that children can access at their own pace. Once this is established children are better able to retain their confidence when experiencing something new. This can also avoid seeing a predisposition to simply following the motions.

13 Nurturing school children to be brave

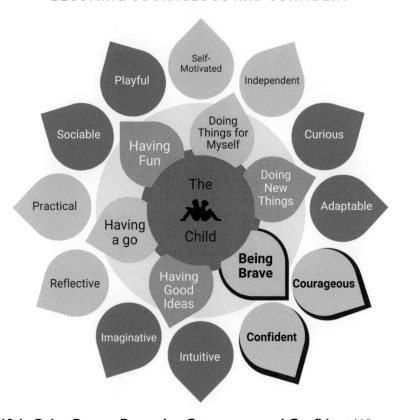

Being Brave

BECOMING COURAGEOUS AND CONFIDENT

Figure 13.1: Being Brave - Becoming Courageous and Confident: When we offer a child opportunities to be brave, they can experience their courage and confidence in ways that permit these dispositions to develop.

DOI: 10.4324/9781003327059-15

In this chapter we are going to focus our attentions on nurturing children to be brave, developing the courage and confidence to feel a greater sense of security and well-being and developing these dispositions ready to support all the experiences to come (Figure 13.2).

When we think of a child's first days, weeks and months in a school classroom we can see the many new experiences that they must manage. If this period of transition is to be a positive one, these experiences must be faced with a degree of bravery that we as adults may at times struggle with. Children need to feel confident enough within these unfamiliar surroundings to persist through the obstacles they will face. Only then will they feel ready to embrace any new opportunities as they are expected to. Taking risks and pushing their boundaries, even when this requires a belief in themselves that may as yet be untested.

They need to feel courageous enough to have a go even when they are no longer in their comfort zone. Trying again when new skills do not perhaps come easy, with the resilience to not let this effect their self-worth. They need to feel secure enough to voice their own opinions and to get involved. And if they can experience every success and setback as a natural part of the learning process, they can then establish a positive sense of themselves that they can take forward into all future learning experiences.

Knowledge

Know why it is important for school children to be brave

Following every major transition in a child's life they will experience a period of being out of their comfort zone. This may be felt as a positive thing, where the benefits that can come from progressing through change can be understood. They may learn to thrive within an environment of challenge, eagerly embracing new opportunities. Or they may become reticent, unwilling to put themselves forward or risk moving beyond the things they are already reasonably good at. Ultimately becoming frightened of feeling unsure.

When we can develop a self-belief within our children they can become capable of facing the challenges ahead. When this is in place children are better able to manage the expectations placed on them and to even choose some of their own. They are more confident to have a go, taking advantage of the opportunities you are offering them, without allowing their nerves to get in the way of what they might otherwise achieve. Developing resilience and credibility, both within themselves and others. And with the courage to move on, they can venture into the unknown, taking on new risks and challenge with the confidence needed to succeed.

When a child feels this confidence within themselves they can learn to understand their own abilities and their value. Along with acknowledging their weaknesses without being frightened of them. They are able to focus on what they can do well, overcoming self-doubt as they take on greater challenges and persist through the obstacles they may face. And they can validate their own efforts, finding a self-assurance and well-being within this that allows them to continue without the need for constant external support or praise.

When this is secure, children can take on the difficult challenges faced when learning to read or making new friends. They can try again when mistakes are made, with the courage to restart, continuing despite difficulties and all in the absence of continual feedback.

Understanding

Understand how to develop a child's ability and desire to be brave in the school classroom

Bravery and the courage and confidence that drive it is a clearly visible persona that confident children become known by. Both to themselves and others. With each experience informing the next, children need positive experiences as they explore things that are unfamiliar to them. Developing the bravery they need to take an active role in all the opportunities available to them. As they find and extend their comfort zone at a pace that is right for them, they develop this understanding of where their confidences lie. But to do this, they need opportunities to try different things, to have permission to venture into areas that interest them, reacting in the moment as they push their own limits and capabilities (Figure 13.2).

Figure 13.2: We want to raise our children to have confidence in their own abilities, with the courage to progress however they wish in their lives. This doesn't come from simply conforming, children need to experience these moments of bravery throughout their learning.

Within this will come an element of risk as children establish the courage they need to move beyond areas they are already confident in. And will at times, naturally come with experiences of failure if they are to experience the depth and breadth of possibilities available. Children then need safe opportunities to securely feel what risk is like, with the independence and permissions to find their own path. This may mean deviating from other children, but if you can support them to explore in ways they personally need to, you are allowing a level of trust to develop within themselves. Along with the personal sense of achievement that follows, allowing them to actively challenge their limits and realise their own ambitions.

A child's confidence grows when you place confidence in them. So if a child shows a lack of it, challenge this perception and instead demonstrate that you have faith in them. You might like to offer them opportunities for responsibility, as you show them that you see them as capable. They will automatically gravitate towards the areas they feel most confident in, so be sure to offer a wide range of activities for them to experience. Once established, a learnt bravery allows children to have a voice, to stand up for themselves and to go after what they want. It will see them embrace opportunities and to be proud of their efforts. But to realise this they need these opportunities and challenges within a safe environment in the first place.

Managed effectively, confidence can develop through both our setbacks and our achievements, both of which are required as you help children realise that confidence is a product of their endeavours, not solely a driver of it. When these experiences are positive ones, children become more ready to take on greater learning challenges. But to do this, they need to feel secure in other areas, within a stable and nurturing environment where they feel these levels of confidence and know they have your secure backing.

Support

Be supported in offering practice, environments and experiences where this can be explored

When we offer children stable, nurturing environments, where a balance of support and independence is offered their sense of bravery can flourish. From this place of security and emotional well-being, we can empower a child's self-belief. Through a range of confidently applied skills and opportunities they can then try different things and voice unconventional ideas and opinions. Being outwardly confident, children learn to stand up for what they believe in and to speak for others with less of a voice. But helping them to feel brave may mean different things to different children. For some it will be taking a risk with a trickier activity, for others it may be speaking up in front of a group.

Within your teaching, look to offer children opportunities to experience risk and challenge. When these are offered through positive experiences, they no longer need to be feared or avoided and through your careful guidance a child can instead develop feelings of well-being and a sense of security. Once this is established, children can increasingly turn their attention to other things and you will notice this as they become more focused. When they feel self-doubt and experience setbacks, they will be more readily able to persist through them. And when you connect this pursuit of a braver response with a personal interest, children are more likely to persevere even through testing times, challenging any expectations that they may feel along the way.

So, as you support children to push themselves further, offer opportunities for them to learn from their mistakes. When you resist being too quick to support, they learn to continue through their difficulties. As you allow them to trial their decisions, stopping only when they feel ready, a personal sense of their own capabilities can develop. And when given permission to fail, strength and resilience are given room to grow, inspiring their determination to come back stronger. So, value setbacks as well as success as you fuel their ambition and drive their future efforts to new heights.

Sometimes children need courage to move away from familiar environments, activities and friends to explore adventures within the unknown. Through experiences that would otherwise not have been possible or freely chosen, children can confront and stretch the limit of their perceived abilities. Learning a wider range of skills and aptitudes that, with further exploration, can become embedded with ease. Within this zone of engaged learning, distractions are more readily avoided and their next steps are more readily pursued as engagement becomes more intense in the active pursuit of a novel goal, whilst also generating a wider scope of experience.

To stand up for what they believe in, children need the courage to voice a personal opinion. So, offer opportunities for them to say what they think, even when this involves an independent view. Not only does this increased confidence to speak up teach them so much in the moment, but it also offers them the belief that they can challenge any barriers placed in the way of them achieving their goals (Figure 13.3).

Figure 13.3: Experiences of voicing an opinion and having these listened to and respected, even when they may be vastly different to what you were expecting, develops the confidence children need to stand up for themselves and what they believe in.

Offer children experiences that allow them to succeed beyond their expectations. This is especially powerful when we give children these opportunities in small groups. Not only do they get the instant feedback, but they are also gaining the respect of the group as their confidence in them grows. As well as significantly bolstering a child's confidence, this also allows them to manage potential negativity as challenges from a peer are more readily accepted and faced.

Whilst confidence develops through effective challenge and risk, being thrust into a difficult experience too early can have a negative effect. So, as you develop children's self-awareness, offer them the confidence and the opportunity to step away from overly difficult situations or those selected in error, learning to distance themselves from unsuitable paths.

14 Nurturing school children to have good ideas

Having Good Ideas

BECOMING INTUITIVE AND IMAGINATIVE

Self-Motivated

Playful

Independent

Sociable

Doing Things for Myself

Having Fun

Curious

Practical

The

Doing New Things

Adaptable

Having a go

Child

Reflective

Having Good Ideas

Being Brave

Courageous

Imaginative

Intuitive

Confident

Figure 14.1: Having Good Ideas - Becoming Intuitive and Imaginative: When we allow a child opportunities to have their own ideas, they experience what it means to be intuitive and to use their imagination, encouraging these dispositions to develop.

DOI: 10.4324/9781003327059-16

In this chapter we are going to focus our attentions on nurturing children as they have good ideas, using their intuition and imagination to develop these powerful tools of learning (Figure 14.1).

When children are given opportunities to have ideas of their own they get to see the power of their own thinking, their imagination and their intuition. As they gain first-hand experiences of seeing this potential within a situation they can see the individual power and impact that they can bring to it, opening new opportunities and taking their thinking to a higher level. At the same time as hearing and respecting the ideas and inspirations of others. When they are granted permission for moments of free expression, children gain meaningful experiences of bringing their own thoughts and ideas alive and the innovation that this can lead to.

But all of this requires positive experiences and permissions. For children to use their own instincts, they need environments where every expected action and response is not predetermined. They need to learn to feel comfortable within situations that perhaps lack specified direction, happy to follow their instincts rather than direction. And they need past experiences to learn by, to inform their next move and to develop their instincts. To achieve this, the possibility of having and voicing their own ideas needs to be a regular part of their learning experience.

Knowledge

Know why it is important for school children to have good ideas

Within a busy classroom it can be a challenge to offer every child the opportunity to express their own ideas, especially when they become keen to tell you their ideas about everything. But it is through these opportunities that children develop their imagination. They experience the potential of their individual thoughts, to see what is working and to challenge what they are struggling to understand. They learn to become a creative influence on their world, along with the sense of possibility that this brings.

Figure 14.2: Engaging in small group work can be a great way for children to have their ideas heard.

With permissions to voice an idea they can be innovative in their thinking, unafraid of deviating from the expected response. They can mentally rehearse their early thoughts about something, figuring things out as they gain deeper understanding. And they can see beyond the expected, learning to find progressive approaches to the problems of the future. All the while, stretching their horizons as they see their own potential and their passions ignited (Figure 14.2).

When the experiences we offer to a child are effectively suited to their ability and current interests, they can become deeply engaged within their pursuits. Trialling different ideas, before seeing their innovations realised and reinventing when things become difficult. Through this process they experience the value and benefits that come from applying their learning. They formulate ways of making connections within their own understanding, adapting to different information, situations and any new ideas that maybe introduced.

When we value a child's unique abilities through these permissions, they learn what it means to be respected as an individual. Through opportunities to use their instincts, they learn the confidence to disagree, as well as to have a different opinion as they learn to make informed decisions. This requires experiences of combining their developing knowledge and experience and so requires lots of both, but once established the ability to have and to express a new idea will take a child's thinking to another level. From a practicing technician to the perceptive and inspired levels of the scientist.

Understanding

Understand how to develop a child's ability and desire to have good ideas in the classroom

Children need no encouragement to have an idea, but they do need the confidence and permissions to express them. They need uninterrupted periods of time to trial and explore their thinking, unafraid of mistakes or deviating from an expected response. Bringing various solutions together, independently and within small groups, as they generate and assimilate new knowledge, refreshing their understanding and discovering diverse ideas.

To promote a desire to do so, children need to be in an environment where they are not overly constrained by expectations. When they are given opportunities to freely explore, they can develop an intuition for what they need to do next. And as they realise their achievements, they can respond to their evolving interests, pursuing alternative routes and taking the "leaps of faith" required for true advancement.

When children become involved in their learning, allowed to hypothesise and deduce reasoning for themselves, their imagination ignites and a sense of personal validation can be realised. When permitted to apply their previous knowledge and to learn from it children can explore potential new outcomes, developing an intuitive sense for what may happen or be needed next. Children do then need opportunities to follow their own instincts as they learn to identify positive situations and beneficial end goals for themselves. And they need opportunities to stand alone as they experience their independent responses and actions towards the things that interest them. For it is in these moments that children are realising their unique abilities and talents and are beginning to form their own opinions. But to develop this intuition requires the development of and trust in their own, inner voice. And to do this, they need to hear it.

However, this level of self-trust and freedom of thought can be severely dampened by the distractions of an end goal, predetermined learning objectives or the clock on the wall. While these things may give the adults structure and guidance, they do little to inspire the abilities of a child and need to be managed. As someone who is aware of the potential within an opportunity, you can aid these explorations by offering a child a degree of autonomy alongside the benefits of a supportive, knowledgeable and experienced other. As you do so, guide them as they explore their unique or revolutionary ideas more fully. You can help them to learn from previous experiences and consider what might work by thinking about what happened last time. Whilst these may need to be appropriate to current need, you can then avoid simply offering a set of instructions.

Support

Be supported in offering practice, environments and experiences where this can be explored

A child's imagination flourishes when they are given opportunities to reinvent that which has become expected. So, offer children a degree of independence, where they can use their imagination to apply processes in diverse ways or to approach problems from new directions. Give them freedoms within their choice of environment and activity as they explore their own goals. With this autonomy children tend to engage deeper, extending their possibilities in pursuit of new and diverse experiences. By not conforming to expectations, they extend their learning as unique and revolutionary ideas, thoughts and pursuits can be trialled. And only when these freedoms are offered can children learn to intuitively adapt their behaviours and responses as needed.

Offer children opportunities to work in small groups as they see the ideas of others, developing a collective respect for each other. By listening to and learning from others, effective and suitable ideas are modelled that children can learn from, as well as developing the confidence to voice their own. You can also use these opportunities to remind children of the previous things they have tried and the insights they have gained. Enhanced through every chance they are given to talk through their new ideas.

Allow children to meet their learning objectives by pursuing areas of personal interest, rather than always following prescribed activities with predetermined outcomes. If you can incorporate a range of different skills for them to develop, they will be making further connections within their learning as they combine, test and apply in innovative ways. For example, they may visualise a number of potential solutions as they plan what to do next, incorporating any number of previous learning insights.

When you introduce a new topic, avoid being too quick to offer an explanation. Instead ponder with the children. When you introduce an unfamiliar piece of equipment, consider what it might be or how it might be used. Where do they think this may have come from? Who might have used it? What could it be for? Then after the discussions, allow them to explore

Figure 14.3: Building a den that can house three children without collapsing may need lots of intuition, instinct and imagination. However many mistakes are made, the learning is always positive.

their ideas, guiding them to any "evidence" or past experiences they can utilise as you help them consider what they may intuitively know (Figure 14.3).

Allow children opportunities to consider and talk through new tasks and any problems they may be facing. You can use these discussions to help children realise that everyone may be experiencing challenges, but that their comments and actions could also help others. You can further utilise and inspire their imagination by giving them opportunities to act on any suggestions that these discussions have inspired.

When mistakes are made, help children to see this as a positive. Familiar with more than one way of completing a task, they will realise that different pathways may allow for different and unique solutions. And when no positives are forthcoming, embrace this as a natural and expected part of the learning process, rather than a negative experience to be avoided next time they do not know something.

15 Nurturing school children to have a go

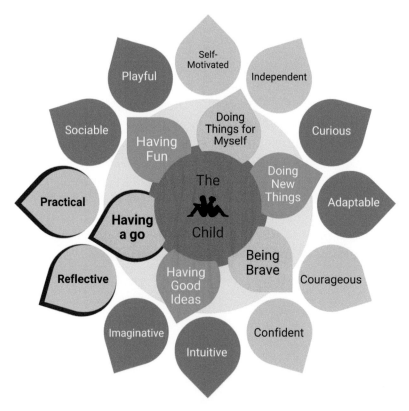

Figure 15.1: Having a Go - Becoming reflective and practical: When a child is given opportunities to have a go for themselves, they can develop a wider range of practical skills and gain the experiences they need to reflect upon as these dispositions develop.

DOI: 10.4324/9781003327059-17

In this chapter we are going to focus our attentions on nurturing children as they develop the abilities and desires to have a go, developing the practical skills that allow them to do so and the deeply impactful opportunities to reflect that follow (Figure 15.1).

There is a reason children are driven to reach out and experience everything for themselves from the moment they are born. These experiential methods of learning are so powerful that they remain with us throughout our lives. When given opportunities to become physically involved in their learning children begin drawing physical and cognitive abilities together with processes that are creating connections deep within the brain. This results in a far deeper understanding and in ways that are remembered and understood.

When children are given these experiences their self-development flourishes as their thinking becomes informed on multiple levels. They are developing the underpinning skills to make sense of what they are hearing and seeing, while experimenting with their understanding, fine tuning it and adding the realism and authenticity that makes it worth remembering.

The trouble comes when children are denied these opportunities. When they are expected to ignore their physical desire to move and instead required to remain still, to listen and understand without the support of all the systems of learning they have available to them. When instead, we could be offering the satisfaction that comes from effective learning processes. Inspiring children to want to know more, as they attain higher levels of awareness, developing a depth of understanding ready for the more complex learning ahead.

Knowledge

Know why it is important for school children to have a go

Without application, children have little understanding of complex concepts. Neither do they have much of an interest in them. However, when given opportunities to have a go at things for themselves, children gain the memories they need to pin their understanding to. They develop the muscle memory of weight before applying it in a physics class. They explore mathematical language in ways that have meaning and purpose. They can experience different compounds and reactions through cause and effect. They are learning how to apply the effort needed to achieve their goals and becoming interested as they see their ideas take shape. And they are seeing the purpose of being constructive, while gaining the insights to inform their choices and decisions (Figure 15.2).

Through these hands-on processes, children are developing the transferrable skills and abilities that they will need to access deeper levels of understanding. Practicing and refining their abilities, while progressing into new areas of learning. They are developing an informed idea of how to proceed with a task when stumbling blocks are encountered, adapting to different circumstances and learning to consider different viewpoints.

When we offer children opportunities to gain first-hand experiences of their own abilities and evolving skills, they can use these to reflect on their outcomes. Driving their self-awareness as they learn from their actions and the instant feedback this offers.

They can check the validity of their decisions as they consider their options from a more informed standpoint. And as they learn to question, they can become aware of important features, patterns and similarities as they make connections in their learning, allowing various threads to come together.

As they become more aware of their growth and areas of potential, children learn to consider previous responses and the feedback they have received. And as they learn to manage this constructively, they become more self-governing and motivated to explore the next opportunity, whilst at the same time knowing when to move on. As this begins to improve their outcomes and drive their progress forward, children can become more self-aware, with strong supportive links to their mental health and well-being.

Figure 15.2: What might look like a childhood activity is steeped in mathematical, scientific and social understanding.

Understanding

Understand how to develop a child's ability and desire to have a go in the school classroom

For children to develop the ability and desire for practical self-development, they need positive memories of having a go at things for themselves. With the freedoms to try, rather than simply observe, children experience the engagement of hands-on learning. And with the autonomy to access the environments and resources needed when they need them, children become familiar with practical thinking as they gain a powerful set of learning tools. However, this approach to learning must be valued and embraced by the influential adults around them. It may take some forward planning as you structure opportunities and make time for the learning potential being offered. And it may require a somewhat different mindset but the benefits are staggering. When we can offer this to children, they can see their abilities evolve through the process. Learning to see themselves as a capable learner as they realise their achievements first-hand and feel their confidence grow.

You can develop this motivation by allowing children to take an idea and consider how they could make it work in practice. This is especially meaningful when they can relate to the authentic and engaging scenario you are considering, such as planning for an event they can attend. Start by offering a relatable situation and invite children to take it in a direction of their choosing, allowing them to discuss their ideas as they make alternative suggestions. You can be on hand to model key skills but let them request additional knowledge or resources, rather than having you anticipating what may be required.

Figure 15.3: Taking an idea, planning it out and seeing how it might work in practice offers deep felt learning that children cannot get from the classroom alone.

Through such opportunities children can experience following their own path, rather than simply completing pre-established tasks as they develop a significant array of new skills. Facing unforeseen difficulties and developing practical solutions, they will be learning to use what they have and adapt. Developing the network of support and new skills needed as they manage an evolving situation (Figure 15.3).

You may need to demonstrate some required skills or offer some introductory knowledge, but pair this with the children's need to embrace such skills for themselves. As their interest is aroused, use this to extend their understanding as you discuss practical ideas, potential explanations and possible solutions. The personal ownership children are gaining of the outcome has widespread benefits as they trial these new competencies that are continually informing their thinking. And as they reflect on these experiences, invite them to consider how they solved their problems, the measures they put in place and the more complete understanding they now have.

Support

Be supported in offering practice, environments and experiences where this can be explored

We know children need first-hand physical experiences throughout their education, along with the permissions to make their own sense of them. This is a deeply rooted learning process as children develop the underpinning skills required. But through these experiences, they are also developing a deeper understanding of how things work so that they can apply their knowledge to a wide range of situations.

You can support children's thinking as they react to practical opportunities by allowing them to explore and re-create scenarios in applied ways. Offer them opportunities to proactively approach and select tasks for themselves. Ensure these tasks invite a repertoire of practical responses, through which children can develop a range of knowledge and experience. You can have guidance and support on hand, but let children identify where this is required.

Allow them to experience individual practical experiences, as well as working in small groups where they can observe and support the practical skills being modelled around them. In these scenarios, children learn to react to multiple issues as they arise. This also allows them to adjust their responses to changing circumstances and different points of view. When you can root these experiences in authentic, real-world applications, children develop skills they can reflect on and apply within familiar situations. As their abilities develop, you might like to add an additional level of realism by seeing how they manage when information or resources are reduced or unexpected.

Children also need time to reflect as they assess the insights they have gained. So, introduce times for discussion, interaction and questioning. Modelled within nurturing environments, children can experience the benefits of seeking a more informed outlook as they themselves value the process of raising informative questions and drawing conclusions. In these sessions children can identify gaps in their own understanding whilst learning not to dwell on areas of development. Within an established structure of reflection, children can consider what has gone well, while contemplating active improvements. With your guidance they can learn to seek alternatives to any automatic responses, whilst developing a greater awareness of solutions that may otherwise not be considered. All the while realising that everyone experiences problems.

Being reflective is an integral part of their understanding. If you can introduce this technique as a continual and eventually subconscious process of thinking, children become better able to identify alternative solutions when they begin to struggle and to consider deeper meanings that may initially be hidden from them. This process is not necessarily automatic and may require some initial encouragement and direction. You can remind them of their previous success, offering a degree of confidence in times of doubt. But children also need opportunities to make and learn from their own mistakes. From these experiences, they learn to modify their actions and consider what needs further practice, ready for those hours of study when an adult may not be so easily on hand.

16 Nurturing school children to have fun

Having Fun

BECOMING PLAYFUL AND SOCIABLE

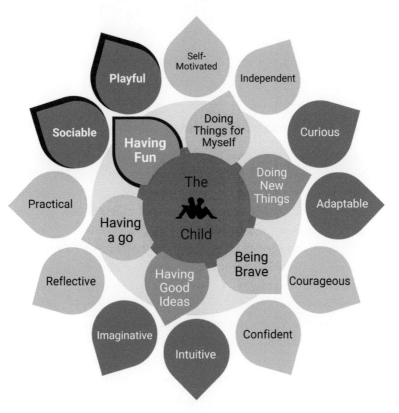

Figure 16.1: Having fun - Becoming playful and sociable: When we offer children opportunities to have fun, they can enjoy the playful and social experiences that having fun means, encouraging these dispositions as they develop.

DOI: 10.4324/9781003327059-18

In this chapter we are going to focus our attentions on nurturing children as they have fun, developing the playful experiences and social encounters that encourage these dispositions to develop (Figure 16.1).

Children are playful, sociable creatures by their very nature. However, times of fun and play are often seen as somehow separate to learning within the school environment. Typically divided by time and space, "playtime" is an activity used to allow children to come together, to use their whole bodies as they become physically active and autonomous in their actions and pursuits. Whilst this tends to be kept very separate from the academic learning of "lesson time," it is the epitome of children's natural methods of learning.

Within playful learning children are permitted freedom from the constraints of reality and the limits of their capabilities. They can imagine greater possibilities, incorporating different ideas and levels of understanding. When given opportunities for physical play and the space to move about children can learn through their whole bodies, as they always have. They are free to pursue an interest in the moment, to engage with others and explore, as they generate new ideas and test them. Social play allows children opportunities to form relationships, developing empathy as they relate to others and in doing so, develop a better sense of self and of belonging within the group. All within a stimulating and motivating atmosphere of fun and enjoyment.

Knowledge

Know why it is important for school children to have fun

Having fun is not simply a treat used to reward children once the important work of learning has been accomplished. It is an integral part of their growth and development that must be valued and safeguarded. That sounds obvious, but when we do not understand and sufficiently value the deeply intrinsic need children have for social engagement and play, it can become forgotten. With some schools effectively scheduling times for play out of the day, using it as a convenient opportunity to catch up on reading, missed work or even to atone for misdemeanours, we must be more mindful of the damage this is having on our children. Especially when it is often the children who need physical play the most that can have it essentially scheduled out of their day.

In play, children experience what it means to be free of constraints. Not held back by what is actually possible, they are permitted opportunities to try, to explore on the edge of their current capabilities. In these moments they get to dream big, to see themselves as strong and capable, taking the risks that lead to great things. Developing the skills needed to mentally rehearse an idea, they are testing scenarios and possibilities as they develop deeper understanding of how things work. Continuously trialling in any manner of combinations, they are making links in their learning, becoming more aware of their surroundings and the possibilities it offers. This is an intrinsic part of creative thinking, but it is also vital in visualising their learning and making sense of it (Figure 16.2).

Figure 16.2: The outdoor environment naturally lends itself to free exploration, deeper engagement and more playful expressions of thoughts and ideas. This can be a natural progression of a young classroom but is no less valuable throughout the school system.

Within social situations children are developing a sense of themselves, establishing a social identity through these childhood experiences that will remain with them. They are learning what it means to belong, how social structures establish and the importance of them. They are experiencing what it means to be a friend, who they can rely on and what being with the wrong crowd feels like. While this may not, on the surface, sound like lessons for the schoolroom, the absence of them is hugely detrimental to a child's well-being, their sense of security within your environment and their ability to concentrate on anything else. And potentially their only opportunity to interact on this level.

Understanding

Understand how to develop a child's ability and desire to have fun in the school classroom

When we look to introduce elements of fun into the classroom, we are looking to establish a freedom from constraints, where exploration and open opportunities are grasped. While guidelines may be present, when play is seen as more than a non-productive break from constructive achievement, a child's minds and their potential can be set free. To encourage this, children need to experience the deeply rewarding and stimulating process first hand. Within nurturing and supportive environments where play is given the affordance of time it is worth.

Through play, you can allow children to envision grander outcomes in ways they have yet to experience. As they engage with different ideas, allow children to explore and connect concepts, seeing what is valid and finding solutions. With deep rooted links to their imagination, these creative thinking processes are effective in igniting a child's curiosity and self-motivation.

To engage with others, children will need to develop their personal skills. These are difficult concepts to master and children need opportunities to practice them. Through experiences of interacting within different social groupings allow children to experience different ages, backgrounds and personalities. As they learn to appreciate alternative perspectives, beliefs and ideas, they are learning to trust in others and to experience the reliability that they themselves can bring.

With the help of their friends, play will facilitate and encourage new ideas and approaches to be generated and considered. As children learn to listen and experience the benefits this brings, they can experience being supported through difficulties, building trust within the group and supporting those with less of a voice. Fuelled through an empathetic understanding of these different suggestions, children can now put forward opinions that are not solely informed by their own experience. Realising the fun and enjoyment involved, benefits are jointly realised, as elements of risk are also shared and valued.

As their ability to develop and sustain healthy relationships establish, children are better able to deal with the difficulties that may arise in play. This might include the ability to remain fair, approachable, amicable and funny, yet on occasion remaining strong when an opinion is challenged. Seeing these skills modelled and then trialling them for themselves is a key part of developing their emotional intelligence. But these are tricky skills for a child to learn and need modelling by the more experienced and practiced within the unpressured arenas of play. When you can offer this with a degree of independence and freedom from adult intervention, children can develop a voice of their own, rather than risk a social awkwardness establishing.

Support

Be supported in offering practice, environments and experiences where this can be explored

As adults we tend to concentrate on the practices we are measured against. Without a metric associated with playful activities it can become relegated, rather than embraced as the powerful method of learning that it is. However, when play is effectively offered, children can experience the motivational elements of humour and fun throughout their learning as a diverse mix of ideas come together.

Offer children different ideas to play with as they combine, test and problem solve in diverse ways. If you can support this with practical activities and real resources, children show a greater commitment and motivation to persist, as the boundaries of their success are extended.

Offer children opportunities to create and explore for themselves within environments where diverse interests are stimulated. When choice of activity, social grouping and environments are offered, unconsidered possibilities arise through a child's playful interpretation. Provided these are valued and appreciated, children can use their initiative to generate new ideas, adapting as discoveries are made (Figure 16.3).

Figure 16.3: Using play, children are able to bring diverse times or realities to life, they can assume a different persona, explore a range of emotions and practice all their skills.

Children need opportunities to mentally rehearse and trial their ideas without commitment. So, with freedom to trial possible methods, let them test validity and durability for themselves. In these moments they can safely challenge the limits of what they have achieved, rather than abandoning attempts for a safer route.

Invite children to voice their thoughts and communicate with thought provoking questions, yours and theirs. As you model and develop their ability to listen and show interest, enhance these playful processes by igniting their active imagination. Offer opportunities to manipulate different ideas through hands-on experiences, playing with the skills they need to develop.

As you introduce difficult concepts, let them explore and experience them through scenarios and strategies that entice them to get playful. Incorporate elements of fun as you use dramatic play to help bring different times and places to life in their imagination. Incorporate practical use of literacy and numeracy, with the resources to write notes, draw maps, solve problems and schedule events.

Begin connecting the language of emotions, feelings and behaviours by talking with them about different social interactions. These can be taken from a period of history, a poem or a game you are playing.

Allow children sufficient time to explore ideas and tricky concepts as they reach their own conclusions. Being sure to give your permissions for play clearly, along with managing any enforced direction towards other things.

And take care not to overlook the motivational importance of bringing fun, joy and laughter into the process. If you want to engage children in their learning, they need to want to do it. So, make it a satisfying experience on a deeply foundational level.

17 Nurturing school children to think

As we draw this book to a close let us revisit the Framework Flower and draw our attention to the magic that allows all of this dispositional development to really take root... and that is in providing our children with the autonomy and permissions to experience what it means to think. To be creative, to simultaneously use different ideas and make connections in their learning, to think of the bigger picture and take logical leaps (Figure 17.1).

Having the ability to think and process ideas is a key part of learning. However and wherever this learning takes place. But to support children to think effectively, we need to be aware of the different styles of thinking and methods of information processing that children need to do with ease. And be ready with the practices and environments that are ready to support it.

Children need to simultaneously combine information from a range of different sources. They then need to use this information to make connections with previous understanding, refining their knowledge to become better informed. Sometimes their learning may call for a logical response as they seek structure, clarifying their thinking in ways that can be tested and relied upon. They may be looking to apply systems or a shared understanding about how things operate. Other times their learning may benefit from a more creative thought process. Innovating as they think in new ways or manage when limitations might get in their way.

To fully realise their capabilities, children need to be open to a wide range of opportunities. Able to embrace their full environment they are ready and able to recognise the diverse possibilities all around. Ready to grasp the potential it offers, rather than becoming limited by a narrow view. And all this begins with their experiences of voicing their thoughts and ideas through all the learning experiences they are offered.

DOI: 10.4324/9781003327059-19

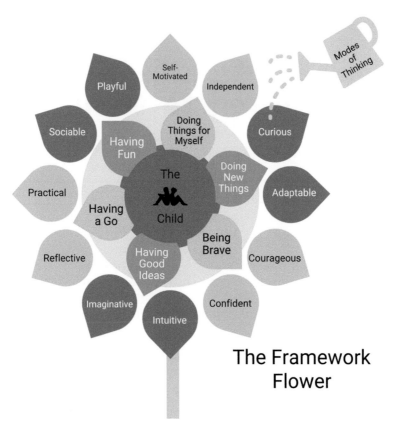

The Framework Flower

Figure 17.1: Nurture the framework flower through independent thought: Throughout all our interactions, provocations and permissions, we need to remember that we are raising independent thinkers, ready to engage and ponder, to understand and know.

Knowledge

Know why it is important for school children to think

Throughout their education children are expected to think in some highly sophisticated ways. They are simultaneously accessing and processing information from various sources, whilst becoming familiar with multiple environments and their expectations. They will be involved in multiple exchanges as they juggle the physical and social demands placed on them, all the while processing new information as they make connections in their learning. Such as knowing individual symbols and sounds, while performing the mechanics of writing, or the logical thought processes needed to demonstrate mathematical understanding.

Solutions to the problems children face will not always be straightforward and their developing understanding may need a range of diverse steps. Through positive experiences of thinking for themselves, children are learning to utilise and respect their creative thought processes. When they know how to combine techniques and access information from wide ranging sources their learning is no longer limited or directed in ways that constrain their potential. Different opinions and sources of information can also be considered. All of which are key thought processes required for more complex principles of later learning (Figure 17.2).

When taking all this learning into the real world, the ability to think and to have a unique

Figure 17.2: Thinking is not always a linear process and may require creative, diverse or simultaneous steps.

thought becomes valued. It is after all an essential part of solving problems and creating something new. However in the school classroom, where conformity can be a more highly praised trait, children can struggle to question or voice their own thoughts. Especially when situated within a large group or when an adult led activity seems to prize only one requested response. However, when children are given opportunities to think for themselves, they experience the power of education. When they are given opportunities to consider their own ideas and suggest a unique response, they learn to recognise their own learning power without feeling mistaken or isolated. And being able to think with the confidence and independence to challenge is a key part of developing deeper understanding and a belief in themselves.

Understanding

Understand how to develop a child's ability and desire to think for themselves in the school classroom

To develop a creative mindset children need opportunities to become engaged in creative pursuits. This takes more than a predesigned art activity; it means embracing their own creativity as they explore new avenues of enquiry. It means discovering their own ideas, even if the outcome is unknown or not always considered favourable. And recognising the value of innovation as their learning introduces new or unexpected information. Creative thinking also allows children to challenge their own understanding, but to do this they need opportunities to question and challenge what they think they know.

Learning is a multifaceted business, combining core pieces of knowledge, understanding and processing in simultaneous ways. Whether this is how different letters interact before reading a word or how to measure the temperature on the playground.

A diverse skill set, children need to be aware of what may be a wide range of information. This might begin with a degree of unease as certain elements are only partially known or if physical and mental manipulation is required. It is only when children are a part of this process that deeply engaged learning can follow. By allowing children to move around the space and question what they think they know, they can go beyond that which is immediately apparent, developing the transferable skills needed for future learning.

The patterns, expectations and structure you surround children with offer a degree of stability in what may otherwise seem a chaotic place. These routines help children navigate their day, especially when environments and demands are new. With this familiarity children can implement their own fact-based, logical assumptions and find their own way through challenges. To develop logical thinking processes children then need opportunities to make connections and draw their own conclusions, enriched through familiar experiences they can relate to. Repeated experiences of using their evidence-based logic will help develop this clarity of thinking, adding structure to their thoughts.

Thinking widely with a depth and range of understanding allows children to explore ideas with an open agenda. As each new experience is encountered it brings with it new understanding and techniques and as lateral approaches are considered, unique solutions and opportunities present themselves. Wider discussions allow for a more enriched world view, opening their minds to alternative ways of looking at things as their thinking is no longer rigid or narrowly focused. Children become better able to visualise alternative solutions and means of making something happen. And encouraged to think wider, children's abilities can be stretched as they embrace difficult concepts in more informed ways (Figure 17.3).

Figure 17.3: How am I going to get the water collected in the sand pit to the mud kitchen at the other end of the playground?

Support

Be supported in offering practice, environments and experiences where this can be explored

Through the opportunities you give children to challenge their thinking, they are learning to query the reasons why. They are developing an empathetic interest in what others are thinking and doing as they learn to consider more than their own opinions. And as you engage a child's desire for knowledge, you can encourage them to dig deeper and explore all possibilities, rather than accepting an offered platitude.

Encourage your children to ask questions and to think around common responses as they seek creative and innovative answers, rather than the way it has always been done. Along with offering some freedom of choice and the potential to find their own solutions to problems that mean something to them.

Offer the information needed for a task in a range of places and formats as children experience multi-tasking and combining their developing skills. Resources may be limited, not as expected or without a clearly laid out plan allowing children to develop their own creative response.

Let children explore a range of options, intuitively deciding for themselves what is important, informed through past experiences. These diverse opportunities allow children a wider context and meaning to their enquiries and the impact their actions and decisions can have.

Have open discussions as you allow children to clarify missing or misunderstood information within their own thinking. During this process, they will be constructing the links, structure and clarity to their understanding. When children do this in small groups they can also experience different thoughts and agendas, at the same time as achieving their own outcomes.

Working in small groups allows children to clarify their own thinking as they benefit from the thinking modelled around them. A group dynamic also supports emotional stability and helps sustain feelings of well-being. Experiencing team dynamics and communication, children learn to incorporate the actions, views and skill sets of others within their own thinking. Along with benefitting from a pool of expertise and experience as a wide range of opinions and outlooks emerge.

Combining logical, structured approaches with some autonomy you can give children a sense of being supported and in control. Repetition and pattern within their environments, routines and expectations give children a sense of normality and proven reliability. This supports them as they compartmentalise their thinking, applying similar experiences to new and complex ideas.

Offer projects that combine different subject areas and locations. The breadth of knowledge this allows supports children as they make connections across diverse disciplines, as well as allowing for a wider understanding. You can also allow children to self-direct as they avoid becoming limited by, what for them, are more inappropriate pursuits.

Final words

Whether you are just developing an interest in how children learn or you have been in the teaching profession for decades, I hope that this book has offered you much to think about as you look to the developing capabilities and endless possibilities of the children in your life. Through this book I have looked to encourage your reflections on your teaching practices, the environments you offer and the interactions you share in ways you may not have been familiar with. We have considered how the responses of children will be informed through years of prior experiences, influencing the memories you now make together as these will in turn inform the experiences they still have to come, perhaps years from now.

But of course no child's learning is solely dependent on your influence. Learning, rooted within a social and cultural context, will see your socially engaging, opinionated and mobile students keen to share their thoughts and opinions on pretty much anything, whether this is with you or their peers. They will be keen to establish their presence within their environments and the individuals they find there with social connections becoming increasingly important. Whilst managing the expectations and potentially novel constructs of the school classroom.

We often think of a child's first day of school as the beginning of their educational journey, but of course children are learning from the moment they are born. With so much to accomplish in such a short period of time, their early years are a continual stream of experiences that children use to construct their understanding of the world around them. They have made connections in their learning, modifying and adapting their understanding as they have made their own meaning, through every opportunity they have been afforded. Whether these have been positive processes of engaging and purposeful discovery, or limited experiences steeped in frustration. This lifelong journey of interconnected development is now influencing every aspect of their growth and development in infinitely unique ways. If we are now looking to nurture and ignite their learning potential going forward, we must be aware of the effects of this history, as

DOI: 10.4324/9781003327059-20

well as understanding the impact we are about to have on them, recognising children as individuals within autonomous learning experiences. But to do this effectively, we must firstly acknowledge children as more complex than a representation of their presenting sum of abilities. We must recognise and embrace their continuously changing characteristics and the fluctuating abilities of a growing, developing individual with ideas they need to question and challenges they feel compelled to embrace.

If instead we focus solely on universally desired outcomes, our children's natural propensities for learning become confused. Limited to academic skills and outcomes within an environment of classroom procedures and assessment, a child's recognised abilities can become confined within these definitions and any genuine understanding of a child's capabilities and achievements fail to be recognised. While some children will thrive on the pursuit of discrete, measurable skills, many do not as they disengage from teaching styles more suited to older classrooms. Negatively influencing their developing identity within the classroom, long-term effects begin to embed, adversely informing their identity as a capable learner. Their opportunities to act independently become more restricted as previous inclinations to make their own meaning, to transform prior understanding and apply knowledge to new situations is seen to decline. And as they adapt their skills to conform within an environment governed through pedagogical expectations, children are seen to disengage from the learning techniques that have served them so well up until this point. A devastating observation when these are after all the most basic of natural human instincts. With clear impact on their time in the classroom, this also has knock on effects within every aspect of their personal, professional and academic lives, effecting their physical health, their social-emotional well-being and ultimate life trajectories.

Childhood offers a finite period of time within our lives and yet it sees staggering change with monumental effect on every facet of our lives going forward. A child's development during this time must be broad, well-rounded and holistic, where their individual, fluctuating and dynamic dispositional approaches to learning are fostered. Children are social, experiential learners, as we all are. They need to express their understanding, to move their growing bodies and apply the learning they are acquiring just in time rather than just in case. They need opportunities to think, to question and imagine as they demonstrate their growing capabilities, to themselves as much as others. Despite this, many curriculums, programmes and approaches effectively homogenise children as they fail to acknowledge the complex constructs residing within any learning or development experience. In this model, driven by prescribed learning outcomes, it is then the child who can be found lacking or not yet "school ready", within systems that fail to reflect children's intrinsic methods of learning.

Whilst formal classroom pedagogies focusing on group learning and the accumulation of discrete skills and knowledge are an intrinsic part of school education, they should be an informed and conscious decision, rather than the default option. 20 years from now, our children will inhabit a world that we cannot possibly predict. To prepare them for this, there are then more useful skills than displays of knowledge that will become increasingly available at our fingertips. Our children need to experience managing new problems within unexpected situations and evolving environments. They need to grapple with and pursue complex concepts, observing how their thoughts and continued efforts can result in success. Children need permissions to be verbal, to express their viewpoints, to show initiative and pursue original ideas. And as they adapt their thinking, applying reason and investigation, they need to have these efforts recognised as they demonstrate their capabilities, to themselves as much as to others. They need to be comfortable exploring alternative directions with courage and insight, together with the ability to offer opinions, to contribute ideas and work collaboratively. And as they encounter setbacks, to do so with a growth mindset, informed by previous experiences of applying the motivation and perseverance they need to succeed, unconstrained by the pursuit of someone else's desired answer.

If we want children to pay attention and persist with challenging tasks, they need opportunities to develop intrinsic motivation for a personal goal. If we expect them to remember new rules and avoid distractions, they need experiences within multi-faceted environments where simultaneous choices are offered and multiple options held in mind while their decisions are applied. If we expect our children to suppress extraneous movement, to sit still and be goal oriented, they need alternative and regular opportunities to move their growing bodies, freely and physically, responding to every instinct within them. As we embrace a child's natural desires to engage, we are better placed acknowledging these highly complex processes of learning and development, rather than becoming frustrated by them.

Learning involves integrated processes of assimilation, as children engage with an idea, think about it, reflect and revisit, utilising all the dispositions of learning at their disposal. With opportunities to trial various responses, reacting with a degree of freedom and learning from a wide range of circumstances, their predispositions towards these tools of learning can develop as children establish notions of themselves as an individual, as well as an established learner. Dynamic levels of understanding are also embedding as children's individual, fluctuating and holistic approaches to learning are being experienced. These can then be both captured and nurtured once we learn to recognise a child's responses within a wide range of variables. Children will be continuously demonstrating their ideas, their intuition and confident approaches to new opportunities within the environments, directives and groupings they are offered. These insights can then inform pedagogies that are mindful of how a child engages, that are capable of capturing their interconnected developments and illustrate the practices that encourage children to become more advanced in their thinking and are in turn, better able to demonstrate their ideas. Only then can we understand the effects we are having as we nurture development of the skills our children will need to function within a society of tomorrow that we cannot begin to imagine today. And as influential adults in a child's life, we do then have the duty and privilege to nurture this ongoing love of learning and its embedded techniques, recognising that there is so much more to a developing child than their set of achieved milestones.

The pedagogical recommendations offered throughout this series are then focused on nurturing these lifelong processes of intellectual curiosity and learning as children continue on their lifelong journey of interconnected development. They look to support the adults around them to actively consider the opportunities being offered and the impact that key experiences are having on a child's developing propensity towards dispositional engagement. As children become more experienced within their environment, engagements and social interactions, they also look to techniques that offer insight into how these are developing.

Through approaches that have consciously removed attention from learning outcomes or the development goals being measured elsewhere, the Nurturing Childhoods Pedagogical Framework (NCPF) and the techniques shared throughout this series of books offers a profound exploration of the growth and development of children. But it does so by encouraging this shift in perspective as we look beyond the "What should we be doing?" of development guidelines and learning objectives, to recognise the "long-term impact we are having on children when we do". Empowering you as you facilitate the teaching styles and environments that nurture the ongoing development of your children. Mindful of their depth of engagement, the behaviours being demonstrated and the outcomes being realised, both in the moment and as these predispositions take root.

But to embrace this new way of valuing a child's achievements, we need to pause for a moment, to ask ourselves about our teaching intentions and what we want to achieve. We need to think about our actions and what informs them, the gifts we want to send our children into the future with and the capabilities that will allow them to thrive. We need to think about how we continue to ignite their love of learning and discovery as they explore more complex ideas in increasingly independent ways. We need to look at opportunities for children to apply their knowledge as their cognitive abilities become more advanced. And by embracing the social and experiential nature of a child's learning styles, consider how they can learn from one another, seeing their learning take shape with opportunities to express themselves through every interaction, stimulation and permitted experience.

By focusing attention on children's dispositional development, the NCPF captures a comprehensive and holistic understanding of children's experiences of learning and development. Shaped through social and environmental influences and governed through the permissions and limitations surrounding them. In doing so, these books then challenge us to view child development in practice as a deep-rooted, continuous process, influenced by the child, their environment and the teaching opportunities being provided. They look at the autonomy a child needs to explore their world and express themselves, both verbally and physically. And the experiences that allow children to make decisions, take risks and develop their sense of belonging, seen, heard and valued for all that they are.

By demonstrating the impact of experience on children's responses, their motivations and their ability to engage, these books also illustrate why so many children can present as disengaged and disconnected from their learning, a devastating observation when this is after all the most basic of natural human instincts. Surrounding children with adults who understand the intricacies of development is then paramount as we think about the messages we send through the experiences we offer. How do we convey our expectations, our limitations and our empowerments throughout the environment? How do we encourage children to explore and what are our reactions when they do? How do we respond to their ideas when they are very different to what we may have been expecting? We do then need to look through more than our adult agendas. We need to imagine what it means to be the child in front of us. How are they feeling in this moment, are they happy and secure within this environment or preoccupied by something that has nothing to do with a learning objective? What responses are they eager to share? And where do they have a choice, a voice and a degree of autonomy? We also need to inspire this level of understanding in all the influential gatekeepers, determining the nature of the learning experienced and how the outcomes being enjoyed are valued.

Through educational discourse, training and ongoing professional development the Nurturing Childhoods approach can be used by teachers, leaders, policy makers and anyone interested in the underpinning significance and potential we have on the life-trajectories of our children. Through parenting courses, groups and online communities, families can also learn to nurture their whole child, harnessing their natural instincts for learning. As we learn to see and nurture the full potential of children by understanding, embracing and facilitating their intrinsic methods of development. While also realising that none of this is possible if we don't first recognise the importance of well-being and its inseparable relationship with a child's environment, engagements and permissions. And in doing so, recognise the profound impact we have on a child's life-long journey through every decision we make.

Throughout this series, I hope to have supported you as you look beyond the curriculums, guidelines and qualifications guiding you to see the whole child. Through the knowledge, understanding and frameworks presented, I want to have inspired you to reflect on your environments, interactions and the experiences you share. And through their truest form of communication, know how your children are responding to your provocations, as you notice their behaviours and the underpinning dispositions they reveal. When we can place children at the heart of our thinking and remain aware of their evolving dispositions we can gain a clear picture of who they are, both in the moment and as you inform every future experience they have to come. When we begin to see the holistic nature of their experiences, we can have a far greater appreciation for the impact we are having as gatekeepers to these experiences. We can recognise how well we entice deep-rooted characteristics through our provocations and how the messages our children receive, both intentionally and otherwise, are informing their sense of self, both in the moment and as experiences that will inform every experience to come.

If you would like more information, please visit nurturingchildhoods.com where you can find a suite of online courses for teachers, practitioners and parents. Along with the Nurturing Childhoods Community, where you can share your experiences and receive tons of support and guidance. I look forward to seeing you there.

Index

Pages in *italics* refer to figures.